THE PARABLES

THE PARABLES

Their Literary and Existential Dimension

DAN OTTO VIA, JR.

FORTRESS PRESS   PHILADELPHIA

COPYRIGHT © 1967 BY FORTRESS PRESS

Library of Congress Card Number 67-11910

ISBN 0-8006-1392-9

First Paperback Edition, 1974
Second Printing, 1977

6552C77   Printed in U.S.A.   1-1392

To Margaret

PREFACE

I should like to express my gratitude to the Duke University–University of North Carolina Cooperative Program in the Humanities and to the Ford Foundation for providing the opportunity to do most of the work that went into this book. Professor R. M. Lumiansky, Chairman of the Program's Central Committee, and Mrs. Peggy Kale, his secretary, were helpful and courteous during my stay at Duke, as were the staffs of the Divinity School and general libraries of Duke University. I am also grateful to the administration of Wake Forest College for its share in making possible a year away from normal teaching duties.

It goes without saying that the flaws in the work are mine. However, I should like to acknowledge my debt to several friends on the Duke faculty for their critical and helpful reading of parts of my manuscript—Professors Hugh Anderson (now of the University of Edinburgh), Thomas A. Langford, Robert T. Osborn, William H. Poteat, and W. D. White (now of St. Andrews College).

DAN OTTO VIA, JR.

Wake Forest College
Winston-Salem, North Carolina
March, 1966

CONTENTS

INTRODUCTION

In view of the passionate concern of contemporary theology to "go beyond"—beyond whatever has been done in the past, however recent—one might hesitate to suggest something which could be interpreted as a going back. In particular, it might be considered uninformed temerity—some would call it an unthinkable retreat[1]—to question the prevailing Dodd-Jeremias position that the parables of Jesus must be interpreted exclusively in connection with Jesus' *Sitz im Leben*. But whether or not it be seen as a going back, precisely what is proposed in this book is a move *away* from a methodology which interprets the parables severely in connection with Jesus' historical situation. This is not, however, a return to allegorizing.

The ground for such a move is the recognition that the parables—or at least a substantial portion of them—are genuine works of art, real aesthetic objects. This recognition runs contrary to the main tendency of New Testament scholarship as it has dealt with the parables. They are usually treated as if they were not artistic or literary works, and sometimes it is explicitly denied that they are, at least that they are primarily.[2]

---

[1] A. M. Hunter, *Interpreting the Parables* (London: SCM Press, paperback ed., 1964), p. 39; Norman Perrin, *The Kingdom of God in the Teaching of Jesus* (Philadelphia: Westminster Press, 1963), pp. 60, 73.

[2] Joachim Jeremias, *The Parables of Jesus*, trans. S. H. Hooke (rev. ed.; New York: Scribner's, 1963), p. 21; Ernst Fuchs, *Studies of the Historical Jesus*, trans. A. Scobie ("Studies in Biblical Theology," No. 42 [London: SCM Press, 1964]), p. 73; Van A. Harvey, "The Historical Jesus, the Kerygma, and the Christian Faith," *Religion in Life*, 33 (1964), 440, n. 31.

Occasionally it is positively remarked that Jesus' parables *are* of an artistic nature,[3] but the full implications of this have not been worked out in dialogue with aesthetic and (non-biblical) literary-critical thought. A start in this direction has been made, however, by Geraint V. Jones in his *The Art and Truth of the Parables*.[4] The present work will attempt a more thoroughgoing demonstration that a number of Jesus' parables are in a strict sense literary and that because of this they are not just illustrations of ideas and cannot have the immediate connection with Jesus' historical situation which is customarily attributed to them.

Part One will assay to work out a methodology for interpreting the parables, based on an existentialist hermeneutic and on literary analysis; Part Two will make the effort to interpret certain of the parables through this methodology. These parables as literary in nature have a certain autonomy (to be fully discussed in chapter 3) and present a configuration of action-and-meaning which is a more fundamental form of expression than are theological concepts; therefore it is proper to consider such parables first on their own terms and only after that to raise the question of their relationship to Jesus' non-parabolic teaching about the kingdom of God, thereby reversing the procedure of C. H. Dodd. In the exegetical section, the parables will not be grouped on the basis of their relationship to some aspect of the kingdom of God or of eschatology but on the basis of their narrative form, thereby altering the procedure of Joachim Jeremias.

This study will accept the customary classification of the parabolic teaching as similes and metaphors, similitudes,

---

[3] For example, Amos N. Wilder, *Early Christian Rhetoric* (London: SCM Press, and New York: Harper, 1964), p. 51; A. T. Cadoux, *The Parables of Jesus* (New York: Macmillan, 1931), pp. 11–12. Cadoux holds that while the parable is a form of art it is not one of the highest forms because of its being harnessed for service and conflict.

[4] London: S.P.C.K., 1964.

parables (in the narrow sense), and example stories.[5] It would be difficult to agree with Jeremias that such classification is fruitless. Although in the Old Testament the one term *mashal* is used to cover these and other forms,[6] that does not mean that the various forms have the same nature and function and that they can be interpreted in the same way. It is no accident that the parables which are amenable to the methodology being developed in the present work all belong to the class "parable" (in the narrow sense) as distinguished from similitude and example story.

It will not be a part of my primary purpose to argue either for the substantial genuineness of most of the parables or for the secondary character (in position and/or content) of most of the concluding interpretive comments as well as of some internal elements. Both of these points have already been adequately dealt with and are generally accepted by New Testament scholarship. There will be no sketch, as such, of the history of the interpretation of the parables;[7] and the steps in the contemporary exegesis of the parables will be retraced only where it is needed to support or to clarify the approach being attempted here. The Scripture locations of parables mentioned or discussed will often not be cited, but such references are given in an index at the end.

The whole effort being made in this book is not meant to suggest that the interpretation of the parables can get along without the rich exegetical contributions made by such schol-

[5] Cf. Rudolf Bultmann, *The History of the Synoptic Tradition*, trans. J. Marsh (based on the 3d rev. German ed.; New York: Harper, 1963), pp. 166 ff.; C. H. Dodd, *The Parables of the Kingdom* (rev. ed.; New York: Scribner's, 1961), pp. 5 ff.; B. T. D. Smith, *The Parables of the Synoptic Gospels* (Cambridge: The University Press, 1937), pp. 17 ff.; Eta Linnemann, *Die Gleichnisse Jesu* (Göttingen: Vandenhoeck und Ruprecht, 1962), pp. 13 ff.
[6] Jeremias, *Parables*, p. 20.
[7] This has recently been done in English in Hunter, *Parables*, pp. 21–41, and in Jones, *Parables*, pp. 3–40.

ars as Dodd, Jeremias, Manson, Michaelis, Fuchs, and Linne-mann. It is being suggested that in the case of certain of the narrative parables the new angle of vision of a more literary approach would enlarge our understanding.

PART ONE

METHODOLOGICAL

1

Parable and Allegory

Despite the importance and continuing influence of his work, Jülicher did not once and for all solve the problem of defining and differentiating parable and allegory. We may note at the outset two of his major points and then go on to consider the problems which they raise: (a) a parable has one point of comparison as distinguished from an allegory, the latter having many images which are related to various aspects of the idea or experience being delineated; (b) this one point is to be given the broadest, most general possible application.[1]

1. The One-Point Approach to the Parables

The emphasis that a parable has but one point of comparison has continued to be widely held since Jülicher.[2] There is one central thought or point, with the details and other elements serving only to enhance that one point; the other elements have no independent significance of their own. This position is maintained with special vigor by Eta Linnemann. She holds that when we draw from the parable a plurality of

[1] Adolf Jülicher, *Die Gleichnisreden Jesu*, Vol. 1 (2d ed.; Freiburg, Leipzig, and Tübingen: J. C. B. Mohr, 1899), pp. 59, 74. Cf. Nils A. Dahl, "The Parables of Growth," *Studia Theologica*, 5 (1951), 133, 135.

[2] It is seen as a basically, but not absolutely, correct insight by B. T. D. Smith, *The Parables of the Synoptic Gospels*, pp. 23–24; A. M. Hunter, *Interpreting the Parables*, pp. 10, 38; Wilhelm Michaelis, *Die Gleichnisse Jesu* (Hamburg: Furche-Verlag, 1956), pp. 14–15. C. H. Dodd (*The Parables of the Kingdom*, pp. 7, 9–10) affirms the point somewhat more strongly.

significant thoughts we may be sure that we have missed the sense which it had for the original narrator. And it is also a mistake to expose correctly the one central point but to set alongside this point other important thoughts which the parable is supposed to mediate to us.[3]

There are two dangers or problems, however, connected with operating within the one-point approach to the parables. One is that important elements in the parable may be overlooked and the meaning of the parable attenuated, which is the case, for example, in Fuchs' interpretation of The Workers in the Vineyard.[4] Fuchs is almost exclusively concerned with the one point of the vineyard owner's kind act and the relationship of this act to Jesus and his understanding of his conduct as God's act. The attitude and fate of the grumbling workers and what these factors contribute to the meaning of the parable as a total configuration are virtually ignored. On the other hand, the interpreter may, unconsciously and in spite of himself, allegorize the parable—attribute independent significance to the parts —while claiming not to be allegorizing. This is the case in Dodd's interpretation of The Wicked Tenants,[5] as Matthew Black[6] has correctly noticed. Dodd sees reflected in the parable the culmination of God's dealing with his people, the death of Jesus, the climactic rebellion of Israel, and God's judgment upon the latter. It would seem that these difficulties are inherent in the one-point approach and that this approach is artificially restrictive; therefore, it is not surprising that it has been widely questioned.

This questioning, as usually understood, amounts to assert-

[3] Eta Linnemann, Die Gleichnisse Jesu, p. 32.
[4] Ernst Fuchs, Studies of the Historical Jesus, pp. 33–36, 154–156; "Bemerkungen zur Gleichnisauslegung," Theologische Literaturzeitung, 79 (1954), 347–348.
[5] Dodd, Parables, pp. 96–102.
[6] "The Parables as Allegory," Bulletin of the John Rylands Library, 42 (1960), 282–283.

ing that Jesus' narratives[7] are allegorical in some sense. Before proceeding any further, then, it is necessary to arrive at a more elaborate and developed understanding of what an allegory is. We must also achieve a provisional working definition of a parable, though a complete definition will not be arrived at until chapter 3.

2. The Nature and Function of Allegory

We should remind ourselves of the obvious point that there is a difference between making an allegory and giving an allegorical interpretation of a story which is not in itself allegorical. A story which is itself allegorical should be so interpreted. But to treat a story which is not as if it were—to allegorize it—can only frustrate the function and intention of the story. James Smart implies that the ancient allegorizer somehow sensed that the meaning which he wanted to find in the text which he was interpreting was not really in it but had to be inserted.[8] This may be doubted, however, for the ancient allegorizer probably believed—even if wrongly—that the earlier text really intended the meaning that he (the interpreter) wanted to find. Heraclitus, the first-century Stoic, maintained that Homer used the method of *allegoria*—"speaking one thing" but "signifying something other than what is said."[9] Thus it may be supposed that the allegorizing interpreter did not believe that he was reading into the text anything foreign; and that would also be true of the early Christian interpreter.[10]

We have been assuming thus far in this chapter that one of

---

[7] Sometimes the neutral term "narrative" or "story" will be used where the issue is whether the stories are parables (in the proper sense) and not allegories.

[8] James D. Smart, *The Interpretation of Scripture* (Philadelphia: Westminster Press, 1961), p. 132.

[9] R. M. Grant, *The Letter and the Spirit* (London: S.P.C.K., 1957), pp. 9–10.

[10] *Ibid.*, pp. 40, 103, 106–107.

the chief formal qualities of an allergory is that each image and detail has a significance of its own or represents something in the meaning, that there are many connections between the allegorical story and what it represents. This view is too widely accepted to need documentation. There is a second basic formal quality which is closely related to the first one and which is probably more fundamental. It is that the structure, shape, and interconnections of an allegory are determined by something outside itself—by its meaning or referent. The structure of an allegory derives from its meaning.[11] Eta Linnemann describes this graphically. It is as if two designs were placed one over the other. The bottom one, which is the meaning or the situation being referred to, gives the shape, while the upper one, the story, gives the color. For example, the situation referred to in The Great Feast (Matt. 22:1–10)—the destruction of Jerusalem by Rome—causes an unnatural wait in the story (22:7) between the preparation of the meal (22:4) and the invitation to the new guests (22:9).[12]

In a study of the nature of allegory by Edwin Honig, the literary critic, there is essential agreement on this point. According to Honig "we find the allegorical quality in a twice-told tale written in rhetorical, or figurative, language and expressing a vital belief." "Twice-told" means that a venerated or proverbial (old) story has become the pattern for a new one. The new story—the allegory—uses figurative language in order that the old and new can be told simultaneously, and the belief expressed is the reason for the retelling.[13] This means that an image or a detail in an allegory is not of importance primarily in itself nor for the story but as an instance or illustration of something in the old story, in the meaning or refer-

[11] Michaelis, *Gleichnisse*, p. 15.
[12] Linnemann, *Gleichnisse*, p. 16.
[13] Edwin Honig, *Dark Conceit* (Evanston: Northwestern University Press, 1959), p. 12.

ent. The allegorist does not begin with an image which suggests a meaning, but he begins with an idea or meaning and looks for an image to represent it.[14]

Honig, again, declares that the allegorist succeeds when his new story does not merely depend on the authority of the old one but achieves a new structure, meaning, and authority of its own.[15] To this it must be said that it is difficult to make an allegory stand on its own feet, that is, read naturally on its own terms. In an allegory the elements in the story not only represent but are identical with their referents; therefore, they behave not according to their own logic or nature but according to the logic of what they represent. This means that an allegory is likely to contain improbabilities too great to be assimilated into the story; it will appear as nonsensical if read on its own terms and will have to be translated into what it represents in order to have sense made of it.[16] For example, in Bunyan's *Pilgrim's Progress* when Christian and Hopeful are in the dungeon of Doubting Castle, "Christian suddenly remembers that he has in his bosom a key called Promise that will open any lock in the castle"; and with it they let themselves out. As Cadoux has pointed out, the story is in every way shaped by "the religious experience which it represents" and apart from it is unintelligible. In the midst of doubts a Christian may be released by remembering the promise of God, but "it would be insulting to ask anyone to believe" that a man unexpectedly imprisoned remembered after some days that he had a key capable of unlocking any door in the prison.[17]

The question which I would finally pose to Honig, however,

---

[14] Philip Wheelwright, *The Burning Fountain* (Bloomington: Indiana University Press, 1954), p. 89; Northrop Frye, *Anatomy of Criticism* (Princeton: Princeton University Press, 1957), p. 89.

[15] Honig, *Dark Conceit*, p. 13.

[16] Cf. Dodd, *Parables*, p. 8; Smith, *Parables*, pp. 21–22; G. V. Jones, *The Art and Truth of the Parables*, pp. 88, 98–106.

[17] A. T. Cadoux, *The Parables of Jesus*, p. 44.

is, not whether it is not very difficult to create an allegory with a really new meaning and structure of its own, but whether it is not impossible. Since the old story—the meaning or referent —is the pattern for the new one and since there must be manifold analogies between them, as Honig has said, are not narrow limitations imposed on the extent to which the allegory can have a new structure and meaning? If, on the other hand, a story does have a new and independent authority, can it be an allegory in view of the fact that, according to Honig, the definitive quality of an allegory is its close relationship to the old story? It is not suggested here that there is no room in an allegory for a new structure and meaning but that this room is very limited.

Because an allegory is dependent on its meaning or referent, the situation to which it relates, the reader must be familiar with the latter in order to understand the story. Thus an allegory can only pass on hidden information to the initiated.[18] Since the reader, in order to understand the allegory, must be familiar with the referent or situation which shapes it, it may be suggested that whether or not a particular story is taken as an allegory depends somewhat on the standpoint of the reader. A reader unfamiliar with the situation referred to in an allegory might miss the intended allegorical meaning—the pattern of references to the old story or the situation to which it relates— and yet find some meaning in the story itself if it has not been too thoroughly accommodated to the old story or situation. On the other hand, a non-allegorical story might be taken as an allegory by a reader who noticed certain coincidental correspondences to a situation with which he was familiar.

An allegory, then, communicates to a person what he already knows, though it communicates it in symbolic and altered fashion. The other side of this is that it conceals its intended

---

[18] Linnemann, *Gleichnisse*, p. 17.

meaning—unless there is an appended interpretation—from those who do not have the necessary knowledge to decipher it. In short, an allegory does not say what it means nor mean what it says, which is what Jülicher[19] meant when he referred to allegory as inauthentic (*uneigentlich*) speech. From the standpoint of the author of the secondary interpretation (Mark 4:14–20) of The Sower (Mark 4:3–9), an allegory (which he takes Mark 4:3–9 to be) certainly conceals its meaning, for no one who heard The Sower could have guessed that its meaning was the one attributed to it in the interpretation. Could any hearer have surmised from the story itself that the birds who ate the seed (4:4) really represent Satan (4:15)?

Since by the time Mark was written the meaning of some of the parables had been obscured or lost, and since it is the natural function of allegory to conceal or obscure its meaning, we can understand how Mark took Jesus' parables to be allegories, as he does in 4:11–12. With this he couples his belief in predestination: Jesus used language which conceals the truth *in order that* certain men might not be able to understand, repent, and be forgiven. Mark is really saying that the parables in themselves are useless. They conceal their intention from the outsiders and also from the disciples, for they are unintelligible to the latter apart from explanation (4:10–11a, 14–20, 34). It has sometimes been argued that Matthew's substitution of *hoti* (13:13) for Mark's final *hina*[20] was intended as a softening of Mark's thought.[21] Matthew would then be saying that

[19] *Gleichnisreden*, Vol. 1, pp. 49, 73.
[20] Vincent Taylor, *The Gospel According to St. Mark* (London: Macmillan, 1953), p. 257.
[21] *Ibid.*; Alan Hugh McNeile, *The Gospel According to Saint Matthew* (London: Macmillan, 1952), p. 190; F. Blass and A. Debrunner, *A Greek Grammar of the New Testament*, trans. and ed. R. Funk (revision of 9th-10th German ed.; Chicago: University of Chicago Press, 1962), p. 187. Sherman Johnson, on the other hand, seems to believe that Matthew essentially reproduces Mark's thought; cf. *The Interpreter's Bible*, Vol. 7 (New York and Nashville: Abingdon-Cokesbury Press, 1951), pp. 410–411.

because the people were dull and insensitive, Jesus taught in parables in the hope that they would understand and repent. This change would therefore imply that Matthew did not understand the parables as concealing language. However, a careful analysis of Matthew 13:13 in the light of the context of the whole of chapter 13 and of the whole Gospel would seem to indicate that Matthew, no less than Mark, regarded the parables as intentionally concealing their meaning. Probably the *hoti* in both 13:11 and 13:13 is causal. Thus Matthew would be saying that because the crowds are lacking in comprehension, the use of the parables makes it possible to keep the secrets of the kingdom from them.[22]

It may be that behind Mark 4:11–12 is a genuine saying of Jesus with a less predestinarian meaning than that contained in Mark's understanding.[23] In any case Jesus could not have agreed with Mark's view of the purpose of the parables,[24] for it is clear that Jesus intended that the parables should have positive results, that the people should hear with understanding. He questions them about the meaning of the parables and tells them to open their ears (Mark 4:9, 30; 7:14; 12:9; Matt. 18:12; 21:28; Luke 6:47; 13:18). In Mark 4:33 we have the pre-Markan tradition that Jesus used parables because the people could make something of them (cf. also 4:21), but in the

[22] For an elaboration and defense of this view of Matthew see my article "Matthew on the Understandability of the Parables," *Journal of Biblical Literature*, 84 (1965), 430–432. Passages from this article are here reproduced with the permission of the *Journal of Biblical Literature*.

[23] Cf. T. W. Manson, *The Teaching of Jesus* (2d ed.; Cambridge: The University Press, 1948), pp. 77–80; Joachim Jeremias, *The Parables of Jesus*, pp. 14–18. Jeremias holds that 4:11–12 did not originally refer to the parables in particular but to Jesus' teaching in general (*Parables*, pp. 17–18).

[24] J. Arthur Baird holds that Mark 4:11 really reflects Jesus' practice, arguing on the statistical ground that many more parables are explained to disciples than to non-disciples. See his "A Pragmatic Approach to Parable Exegesis," *Journal of Biblical Literature*, 76 (1957), 205–206. But he concedes that the correctness of his view depends on whether or not the Gospels' indications of audience are correct (p. 207), which is very doubtful in view of the work of Jeremias (*Parables*, p. 40) and others.

9

very next verse (4:34) a reflection of the opposite (Markan) view (as in 4:11–12) that the parables had to be explained.[25] Beyond this it is contrary to the very nature of a parable that its purpose could be to conceal its meaning.

Yet the meaning of a parable is not always crystal clear or obvious, as is sometimes claimed.[26] A parable is not simply an example or illustration of a general idea which makes the latter easier to understand. According to T. W. Manson[27] this mistaken idea is a Western notion going back to Aristotle. In the Old Testament the term *mashal* is sometimes associated with the term *chidah*, a riddle or perplexing saying (Pss. 49:4; 78:2; Prov. 1:6; Ezek. 17:2). In some cases the meaning of a parable may be left not immediately apparent in order to force the hearer to thought,[28] and this could be a part of what lies behind Mark's superimposed view in 4:10–12.

It is true that Jesus' parables draw upon the familiar world,[29] but the familiar is used in a new way. Thus old ways of thinking are challenged, and resistance to change may impede understanding. Seen in this way a parable may be hard to understand more because of the existential situation of the hearer (cf. chap. 2) than because of any hidden meaning (in the allegorical sense). In addition to this there is a sense in which literary art is "dumb" and needs to be interpreted,[30] but that again is not grounded in its being allegory (cf. pp. 93–94).

[25] Cf. Cadoux, *Parables*, pp. 17–19; Sherman E. Johnson, *The Gospel According to St. Mark* (London: A. and C. Black, 1960), p. 96.
[26] Günther Bornkamm, *Jesus of Nazareth*, trans. I. and F. McLuskey and J. Robinson (based on 3d German ed. of 1959; London: Hodder and Stoughton, and New York: Harper, 1960), p. 69; Hunter, *Parables*, pp. 13–14. Hunter qualifies this position.
[27] *Teaching*, pp. 57–58.
[28] W. O. E. Oesterley, *The Gospel Parables in the Light of Their Jewish Background* (New York: Macmillan, 1936), p. 5; Jones, *Parables*, p. 60; C. E. B. Cranfield, *The Gospel According to Saint Mark* (Cambridge: The University Press, 1959), p. 159.
[29] Bornkamm, *Jesus*, p. 69.
[30] Frye, *Anatomy*, pp. 4–5.

3. Parable, Similitude, and Example Story

We are now at the point of needing to say something more systematic about the formal nature of a parable. Of Jesus' utterances only some twenty-two are called parables, and of these only four are in words attributed to Jesus (Mark 4:13; 4:30; 13:28; Luke 4:23).[31] It is generally agreed by New Testament scholarship that comparison lies at the heart of a parable. Parables are in various ways elaborated comparisons, and this is a feature which Jesus' parables share with some of the *meshalim* of the Old Testament[32] and, also, with the parables of the Greek tradition.[33]

Among Jesus' parables (in the broad general sense) which are more elaborate than single figurative sayings (similes, metaphors, paradoxes, et cetera) there are three major classes: similitude, parable (in the narrow sense), and example story.

A similitude presents a typical, familiar, recurring, everyday scene with more than one verb, usually in the present tense, although the future or the aorist subjunctive may appear. For example, it is typical that a woman with little money, who lost one of her ten coins, would make every effort to find it and would rejoice when she succeeded (The Lost Coin). In a parable we have, not the relating of a typical, recurring incident, but a freely invented story told with a series of verbs in a past tense. The parable is not concerned with what everyone typically does but narrates a particulate thing in which some person or persons were once involved. The similitude gets its force from its appeal to what is universally acknowledged, while the parable achieves its power by making the particular credible

---

[31] Cf. Manson, *Teaching*, p. 63. The "parables" referred to in these four passages are not all parables in the same sense.

[32] The note of comparison is sometimes but not always present in the Old Testament *mashal*. Cf. Smith, *Parables*, pp. 3 ff.; Oesterley, *Parables*, pp. 3–4.

[33] Aristotle *Rhetoric* 2.20.

11

and probable.[34] This last point should not be pushed too far, however, for at least in the case of a Christian parable one of the tests of its effectiveness is whether it can assimilate the improbable without bursting the story. Although the differences between a similitude and a parable can be clearly stated, that does not mean that each story can be easily classified, because overlapping and mixing may occur.

Most of the formal characteristics of a parable mentioned in the preceding paragraph belong to the example story also, but in an example story the symbolic, figurative, or indirect element is missing. In a parable we have a story which is analogous to, which points to but is not identical with, a situation or world of thought outside of the story. In an example story, on the other hand, the meaning or thought or reality with which the story is concerned is not pointed to but is present in the story. The story is an example of it directly and only needs to be generalized.[35] We might say that an example story is like a parable in that the meaning is present in the story itself and it need not be read in the light of another frame of reference in order to be understood, but it is like an allegory in that comparison or analogy tends to have given way to identity and the intended meaning completely shapes the story. The behavior and attitude sketched in The Good Samaritan and The Rich Fool (example stories) are not comparable to or analogous to what a man should do or avoid but are exactly what he should do or avoid. The difference between a parable and an example story may be further clarified by a comparison. The Prodigal Son (a parable) is a freely-invented story about a father and two sons which is somehow analogous to Jesus' own situation

[34] Cf. Rudolf Bultmann, *The History of the Synoptic Tradition*, pp. 170–176; Linnemann, *Gleichnisse*, pp. 13–14; Dodd, *Parables*, p. 7; Smith, *Parables*, p. 17; Vincent Taylor, *The Formation of the Gospel Tradition* (2d ed.; London: Macmillan, 1949), p. 101.

[35] Bultmann, *Synoptic Tradition*, pp. 177–178; Linnemann, *Gleichnisse*, pp. 14–15; Smith, *Parables*, p. 18.

vis-à-vis the publicans and sinners, on the one hand, and the Pharisees, on the other. Moreover, the completely *human* relationships in the parable are somehow analogous to two kinds of divine-human relationship. In The Pharisee and the Publican (an example story), however, the two types of men appear directly; and their respective attitudes toward God and God's action toward them are directly described rather than symbolized as human relationships.

This means that example stories are less different from propositional theological statements than the parables are. For the most part they lack the development in plot and in dramatic encounter which is found in a number of the parables. They also lack that "distance" from their meaning, or point, or from the world of thought outside the story, which is characteristic of a real aesthetic object—and of certain of the parables. Since it is chiefly these matters with which I am concerned in this book, the example stories will not be discussed.

4. The Criticism of the One-Point Approach in Modern Scholarship

We are now in a position to consider more carefully the problem of the one-point approach to the parables. Do some or many of Jesus' stories have more than one point of interest? If so, does this make them allegories and not parables? That is to say, is the possession of one—and only one—central point an inherent formal quality of a parable, one of its differentiae? We may look first at three related but different criticisms of the one-point method of interpretation which have appeared in modern scholarship.

(1) The rigid distinction between parable and allegory on the basis of whether there is one or many points of comparison is arbitrary because a careful consideration of Jesus' stories shows that intermediate or mixed forms do occur. A particular parable may have one central point and also have other ele-

ments that call for consideration. An allegory corresponds at more points than a parable to the old story or the situation being referred to, but the dividing line is hard to draw; therefore, the difference is one of degree, not of kind.[36]

According to Dahl the most important factor in this connection is the recognition that a number of parables are not simply pictures derived from nature or common life but are modeled on traditional metaphors (God as father, king, or judge; salvation as a feast or wedding). Dahl goes on to say that such usage does not make a parable an allegory, but he does maintain that it modifies Jülicher's rigid consistency.[37] Bultmann[38] is evidently not willing to concede this much. In his view the use of such an image as father or king is not allegorical but simply metaphorical; however, Hunter[39] is certainly right in pointing out that any element in a parable which had a symbolic meaning in the Old Testament or in Jewish theology would have been understood by Jesus' audience as carrying that symbolic meaning. This is an allegorical factor.

At this juncture I would draw the provisional conclusion that at least some of Jesus' parables exhibit allegorical features. It is impossible to prevent a *number* of elements in such parables as The Prodigal Son, The Workers in the Vineyard, or The Wicked Tenants from having a certain independent significance. And when we have the image of king (The Unforgiving Servant) or father (The Prodigal Son), the parable is retelling to some degree the "old story" of Israel's history in which God was active as father and king. That does not mean,

---

[36] Cf. Michaelis, *Gleichnisse*, p. 15; Cranfield, *Mark*, p. 159; Grant, *Letter*, pp. 42–43; Jeremias, *Parables*, pp. 18–19, 88–89; Jones, *Parables*, pp. 24–25, 29–30, 78; Smith, *Parables*, pp. 23–24; Amos N. Wilder, *Early Christian Rhetoric*, p. 81; Taylor, *Gospel Tradition*, p. 103.

[37] Dahl, "Parables," pp. 136–137.

[38] *Synoptic Tradition*, p. 198.

[39] *Parables*, pp. 95–96. Hunter (*ibid.*, pp. 38, 95, 114–116) would also seem to be right, as over against Bultmann (*Synoptic Tradition*, p. 198), in holding that rabbinic parables sometimes exhibited allegorical features.

however, that such parables *are* allegories, because it is possible for a parable to absorb allegorical features in such a way that the parable functions finally as a parable and not as an allegory. I would therefore agree that the distinction between parable and allegory is a relative one, but the criterion of difference is not the quantitative one of how many points of comparison there are between the parable and its referent.

(2) The second criticism of the one-point approach says, not that mixed or intermediate forms occur in Jesus' teaching, but that a number of Jesus' parables are allegories. J. Arthur Baird maintains that there are eleven semi-allegorical parables, and by implication he extends this to fifteen.[40] Baird correctly observes that a parable is cohesive,[41] but the parts of the parable are prevented from cohering by his allegorical interpretations. As we move through his interpretation of The Unforgiving Servant, for example, we are told that the king is God, that being his servant represents fellowship with God in his household, that the debt is the sin which drives a man from God's fellowship, and that the threat to sell the wife and children represents the fact that sin implicates one's loved ones.[42] Baird, therefore, has not really seen the parable as a cohesive story. The parts, for him, cohere not with each other but in some detail with a theological framework outside of the story.

Matthew Black rejects the extravagant allegorical interpretations of the pre-critical period in biblical scholarship, but he also rejects as arbitrary the view that Jesus never taught in allegories. The Wicked Tenants he takes as a thoroughgoing allegory and also as a word of Jesus. The violent acts of the tenants represent the rebelliousness of Israel throughout its

[40] J. Arthur Baird, *The Justice of God in the Teaching of Jesus* (Philadelphia: Westminster Press, 1963), pp. 26–28, 63, 260, n. 1. By semi-allegorical he means allegorical but not in the sense that *every* point has an independent meaning. Cf. his "Pragmatic Approach," p. 203.

[41] Baird, *Justice*, pp. 26–27.

[42] *Ibid.*, pp. 64–65.

15

history which reached a climax in the ministry of Jesus. The servants represent the prophets and the son, Jesus. In The Prodigal Son the prodigal is a symbol of the publicans and sinners, and the elder brother, a symbol of the Pharisees. The father is an image of God. Black also holds that The Sower and The Good Samaritan are allegories.[43]

While it is true that certain of Jesus' stories *may* be taken as allegories, it would seem that the more important question is whether they *require* to be so taken. I have yet to demonstrate that those stories which will be dealt with in this book do not require to be taken as allegories but require rather to be taken as parables, but assuming for the time being that it can be demonstrated, I would conclude that those stories which do not *need* to be taken as allegories *ought* not to be so taken. This is because the function of a parable is more significant than that of an allegory. To the extent that a parable is treated as an allegory it is restricted in the exercise of its proper function and is made to function like an allegory. That is to say, it becomes a story which hides its true meaning or communicates to the informed what he already knows. Thus it becomes a vehicle for the exposition of the interpreter's already held ideas.

(3) Cadoux denies that Jesus' parables are allegories, but he also denies that there is only one point of contact between the parable and that with which it is analogous. As long as the story is not unnaturally shaped by its similarity to its referent, the more points of contact there are the easier it is to transfer judgment from the situation depicted in the parable to the situation outside with which the comparison is made.[44]

We may agree with Cadoux that the resolve to find only one point of comparison has the unfortunate results of unduly sim-

[43] Black, "Parables," pp. 276, 281–285.
[44] Cadoux, *Parables*, pp. 50–52.

plifying the judgment to be made and of reducing the parables to "figuratively enjoined platitude[s] obscured by unnecessary ornament."[45] But does Cadoux avoid—as he intends—turning the parables into allegories? He has stated that an allegory has many points of contact with and is shaped by the experience which it represents whereas a parable is an organic unity and has a certain distance from its referent. Allegorizing the parables thus dissolves their unity into separate items.[46] But when Cadoux attributes to the parables multiple points of contact with their referents, he threatens to fracture their unity and to overcome their distance from their meaning or referent. And the threat is carried out, for example, in his interpretation of The Unjust Steward. Cadoux's speculation about whether the steward was really wise, and his association of the steward with the Jewish priests who curried favor with the Romans (the debtors in the parable),[47] certainly dissolve the unity of the parable by connecting the elements with outside realities. And the connections are so strange that if they had really been intended they could only have been made in an allegory which *identified* the steward with the priests and the debtors with the Romans, and then made the identification known through an appended explanation or interpretation. Thus Cadoux does not avoid turning the parables into allegory.

This part of the discussion may be concluded very briefly by saying that while the meaning of Jesus' parables cannot be restricted to one central point of comparison, that does not mean that they are allegories. Thus the possession of only one central point is not one of the essential differentiae of a parable. We must seek a non-allegorical approach to the parables other than the one-point approach.

[45] *Ibid.*, pp. 51–52.
[46] *Ibid.*, pp. 46, 52, 53.
[47] *Ibid.*, pp. 134–136.

17

5. The Parables as Reflections of Jesus' Concrete Historical Situation

Having criticized Jülicher's first thesis—that a parable has only one point—we turn now to the questioning of his second thesis: that a parable's meaning is to be given the most general possible application. The Talents, according to Jülicher, teaches faithfulness in all that God has entrusted to us. The rewarding of faithfulness and the punishment of laziness are found continually in our lives.[48]

Over against such an approach it has been pointed out that this kind of generalizing can occur only by isolating the parables from their context in Jesus' historical situation.[49] We must recognize that Jesus' world is strange to us, and only if we become acquainted with it and see the parables in the light of this world can we understand their real meaning.[50] Jesus did not come to set out a series of moral generalities but to proclaim an eschatological crisis, and this crisis gave to his ministry the character of a conflict. The proper interpretation of the parables is the one which reflects in a very particular way Jesus' eschatological message and the conflict of his ministry, and the meaning seen in the parables must be congruous with Jesus' non-parabolic teaching.[51]

It may also be held that to understand Jesus' parables it is essential to recover and reconstruct the precise, concrete situation in which the parable was uttered and to know what ideas were being illustrated.[52] Beyond this it may be claimed that a right understanding of the parables requires a knowledge of the thoughts, ideas, and value judgments operative in the hearers as well as a knowledge of the author's position. This is because

[48] Jülicher, *Gleichnisreden*, Vol. 2, p. 481.
[49] Dahl, "Parables," p. 135.
[50] Michaelis, *Gleichnisse*, p. 11.
[51] Dodd, *Parables*, pp. 13–19; Jeremias, *Parables*, pp. 11, 19, 21; Cadoux, *Parables*, pp. 12, 26; Fuchs, *Historical Jesus*, pp. 35–36.
[52] Jeremias, *Parables*, pp. 22, 169.

the parable reflects a conflict between the author and his audience and is his effort to elicit from the hearers a judgment, to bring them to agreement with him. He is not trying to reduce them to absurdity nor to beat them back with surface arguments but rather to reach the depth of the conflict in order that a genuine decision might be made. Thus because the parable has such an inherent grounding in its situation of origin, it can be understood only in the light of what it gave its original hearers to understand.[53]

We should notice, however, that the very effort to rule out allegorizing, the reading in of foreign ideas, by understanding the parable in the light of its historical situation[54] may, ironically, lead to allegorizing. In the case of Ernst Fuchs his primary concern with the historical situation influences both his understanding of the nature of a parable and also his exegesis (sometimes) in what I will have to call a strange way. In his view the *tertium comparationis*, A, is to the image part (the parable itself), B, as it (A) is to the material part (the situation-as-meaningful which the parable refers to), B'. He then goes on to say that the material part is the basis for the image part so that "we can work back from the image part to the material part."[55] There is a sense in which the last clause of the previous sentence is correct (see p. 20); but when he says that the parable story (image part) is based on the situation to which it refers (material part), he is turning the parable, by definition, into an allegory. Recall that Honig defined allegory as a twice-told tale which retells an old story, the old story being, in Fuchs' terms, the material part.

This allegorical tendency is exemplified in Fuchs' treatment of The Treasure in the Field and The Pearl Merchant. He comes to the conclusion that the meaning of the strenuous

[53] Linnemann, *Gleichnisse*, pp. 30–31.
[54] Cf. Fuchs, "Bemerkungen," p. 345.
[55] Fuchs, *Historical Jesus*, p. 126.

19

action in the parables is for Jesus' hearers "that they should do nothing." The parable in describing activity paradoxically "says the opposite of what is meant," but Jesus' hearers would grasp his real meaning because they already knew that he meant to speak about God and knew whom Jesus considered worthy of his company and whom not.[56] That is, Jesus associated with the publicans and sinners, who had "done nothing" as far as legal righteousness was concerned. Fuchs, then, draws the meaning of the parable from Jesus' conduct and from the Old Testament understanding of God's loving action—which requires only non-action from man[57]—rather than drawing the meaning from the parable itself.

Surely it is more natural to suppose that the meaning of these parables for Jesus' hearers in their situation involved in some way a call for action or resolve, even though the point be that the effort is evoked by the splendor of the discovery rather than simply demanded.[58] This, moreover, would accord with the inseparable union of the imperative with the indicative which is found in much of the New Testament and would agree with Fuchs' own comments on Matt. 25:31–46.[59]

It is true that we should move—as Fuchs says—from the image part to the material part. Otherwise there would be no point in Jesus' having told the parable. But the material part which the parable yields is an understanding of some aspect of Jesus' ministry which is not wholly available except in the parable. Fuchs really moves to the image part from the material part— in the sense of Jesus' ministry as known outside of the parable —in that he imposes on the parable elements from the historical situation which distort the parable and thus prevent it

[56] *Ibid.*, pp. 126–129.
[57] *Ibid.*, pp. 129–130.
[58] Jeremias, *Parables*, pp. 200–201.
[59] Fuchs, *Historical Jesus*, pp. 111–112.

from being a parable. That is, he prevents it from being a *new* word about Jesus' situation.

Fuchs has criticized allegorizing and decried the attribution of secret meanings to Jesus' parables,[60] but he sometimes does just what he has criticized, though his comments are often incisive. If he is right about his interpretation of The Treasure and The Pearl Merchant, we would have to agree that Mark is right in his view of the nature and function of the parables: they are such that the people hearing, alas, could not understand.

6. A Critique of the Severely Historical Approach

The strange conclusions which may be reached when a parable is allegorized by making its meaning derive from the historical situation might lead one to question the rigorously historical approach, though there are also more substantive reasons for doing so. While one would not want to argue for a methodology which completely ignored the *Sitz im Leben*, some modification of the present tendency seems called for.

(1) The first criticism is that in view of the non-biographical nature of the Gospels it will usually be difficult if not impossible to ascertain in exactly what concrete situation a parable was uttered.[61] The moderate view of Dodd[62] that we will often have to be content with relating a parable to Jesus' situation as a whole is more convincing, and we may agree with Käsemann that while we do not know the exact circumstances of the parables' utterance we do know the eschatological orientation of Jesus' message from which the parables should not be ab-

---

[60] *Ibid.*, pp. 73, 140.

[61] Cf. Henry J. Cadbury, "Soluble Difficulties in the Parables," *New Testament Sidelights* (Hartford: Hartford Seminary Foundation Press, 1960), p. 118.

[62] *Parables*, p. 14.

stracted.[63] But this does not mean that elements from Jesus' ministry or teaching may be imposed on the parable. We must rather begin with the parable itself.

(2) The severely historical approach ignores the basic human element in the parables. They say something to and about man as man and not just to and about man in a particular historical situation. As Bornkamm has pointed out, Jesus' parables are aimed straight at the hearer and do not demand knowledge, education, theoretical judgment, or goodness. Jesus presupposed only man himself in the "unadorned reality of his world."[64] Yet, as we have noticed, the meaning of the parable was not always immediately clear to Jesus' contemporaries. Nor can we ignore completely the difference between Jesus' situation and ours, which creates a problem for translation.

(3) In the hands of some of its practitioners the historical approach threatens to leave the parables in the past with nothing to say to the present. It is perhaps not so much that these exegetes believe that in principle the parables have no relevance for the present as it is that they simply have not given their attention to the problem of translation. Dodd believes that the parables may be ever applied to new situations, but he has concerned himself with their original import.[65] There are practical differences, if not differences in principle, between biblical, systematic, and practical theology; but it would appear that biblical theology should at least concern itself with what it is in the texts that can be related to later situations and how it can be translated. It seems, therefore, an undue restriction on the goal of exegesis when Dodd, in his interpretation of The Talents, seems to be more concerned with identifying the

---

[63] Ernst Käsemann, *Essays on New Testament Themes*, trans. W. J. Montague ("Studies in Biblical Theology," No. 41 [London: SCM Press, 1964]), p. 45.
[64] Bornkamm, *Jesus*, p. 70.
[65] Dodd, *Parables*, p. 157.

counterpart of the one-talent man in Jesus' *Sitz im Leben* than with expounding the implications of the action and attitude of this same man within the context of the narrative of The Talents,[66] though the latter interest is not altogether missing in Dodd.

Geraint V. Jones is sensitive to this danger of divesting the parables of contemporary meaning, and points out that the form-critical search for the *Sitz im Leben* endangers the extension of a parable's meaning to a situation different from the original one.[67] It must be rejoined, however, that it is important to seek the parables' original meaning in their own setting, though elements from the setting must not be imposed on the parables. And against Jones it must be said that seeking the life setting does not in itself restrict a parable to the past. The question is what the next hermeneutical step should be. Moreover, we see that Jones' real problem—ironically in view of his desire to make the parables contemporary—is not the form-critical method but his belief that a number of the parables *themselves*, by their very content, restrict themselves to the past. What relevance does The Talents have for us, he asks, in its reference to the pious Pharisee who "hoards" the law? And since the kingdom has come, the parables which proclaim the coming kingdom are merely *historisch*, that is, past for us. Therefore, something must be added to such parables if they are to be made *geschichtlich*, contemporary and relevant. We must "do something to them," that is, introduce an element of allegory.[68]

This is to misconceive the problem. What is needed is a hermeneutical and literary methodology which can identify the permanently significant element *in* the parables and can elaborate a means of translating that element without distorting the

[66] *Ibid.*, pp. 118–119.
[67] Jones, *Parables*, p. 38.
[68] *Ibid.*, pp. 39, 161.

original intention. It will then not be necessary to allegorize or to add anything.[69]

(4) The severely historical approach ignores the aesthetic nature of the parables and annuls their aesthetic function. Expressed in the broadest possible way the historical approach focuses on the historical context as a clue to the meaning of the parables while a recognition of their aesthetic quality would focus on the parables themselves. I agree with Linnemann and the form-critical approach that in order to understand the parables we must go back behind the Gospels.[70] But the goal of historical and literary criticism is to be able to take any text on its own terms. In the case of the parables this goal is better served by recognizing their aesthetic nature than by first of all deriving their meaning from the historical context or by making them illustrations of ideas.[71]

7. Toward an Aesthetic Definition of Parable

What finally is the most far-reaching distinction between parable and allegory? It is not the difference between one point of reference and many, but, rather, the differing ways in which the elements in the story are related to each other and to the real world or world of thought outside of the story. We have seen that in an allegory there are many references to an "old story." This old story may be literally an earlier story or it may be a world of thought or a historical situation. The elements in the allegorical story refer directly to—are even identified with—the elements in the old story so that the structure of the

---

[69] Bultmann (*Synoptic Tradition*, p. 418) interestingly sees no conflict between the historical approach of Dodd and Jeremias and the generalizing method of Jülicher. The concrete situation would afford opportunities to imprint universal truths on the mind. Bultmann's overall existentialist outlook, however, distinguishes itself from Jülicher's generalizing ideas. T. W. Manson (*Teaching*, p. 64) also sees the giving of a general truth as the main purpose of a parable.

[70] Linnemann, *Gleichnisse*, p. 53.

[71] As in Jeremias, *Parables*, pp. 115, 123.

allegory is determined by its relationship to the latter. Since the features in an allegory are related directly to an outside world, they are related more or less loosely to each other. How a parable differs from this will be indicated briefly below by anticipation and developed in chapter 3. This implies that a parable is aesthetic in a way that an allegory is not.

There is more than one important element in a parable, and all of these features must be given consideration, but they do not relate primarily and in the first place to an event, events, or ideas outside of the parable. They relate first of all to each other within the parable, and the structure of connections of these elements is not determined by events or ideas outside of the parable but by the author's creative composition. Even though the parable may contain images which have inescapable symbolic significance which they bring from another world of thought, this is made secondary to their fusion into the internal coherence of the parabolic story. Neither one nor many of the elements point directly and individually out of the story. That is why the one-point approach is only less allegorizing in degree than the old pre-critical allegorizing: it breaks the internal coherence of the story. The many elements of the parable *within* their pattern of connections as a *whole* do imply an understanding of existence which may be related in some way both to the world of ideas outside of the parable and to the historical situation in which it arose.

2

Parable and the Problems of Theological Language

Because the parables are a special kind of linguistic form, and because contemporary theology and philosophy are particularly concerned with the nature and function of language and with the relationship of language to understanding, it seems appropriate to discuss the parables in relation to the present debate. In doing this the attempt will be made to carry forward the discussion of three questions raised in chapter 1: (a) What is in the parables to be translated, that is, transmitted to us? (b) How is this translation accomplished? (c) What is the goal of translation?

1. Hermeneutic as the Focal Theological Problem

Hermeneutic is the theory and practice of interpreting and understanding language, texts, or the products of human activity.[1] It may well be agreed that the hermeneutical principles to be applied to the texts of the Bible are not different from those applied to other kinds of literature,[2] yet the bibli-

---

[1] Cf. Rudolf Bultmann, "The Problem of Hermeneutics," *Essays Philosophical and Theological*, trans. J. C. G. Greig (London: SCM Press, 1955), p. 235; Gerhard Ebeling, "Word of God and Hermeneutic," trans. J. W. Leitch, in *The New Hermeneutic*, ed. James M. Robinson and J. B. Cobb, Jr. (New York: Harper, 1964), pp. 85, 88, 89, 95, 97–98; Wilhelm Dilthey, *Pattern and Meaning in History*, trans. and ed. H. P. Rickman (New York: Harper Torchbooks, 1962), p. 43.

[2] Bultmann, "Hermeneutics," p. 256; Ebeling, "Word of God," pp. 88–89.

26

cal understanding of history does make the hermeneutical task more urgent for Christian theology than it need be for other basic perspectives. The Christian church believes that history is moving in a definite direction and not simply in repeated cycles and that, although certain similarities and patterns may be discerned, each event has its own irreducible particularity. The present life of the church is seen as derived from a complex event of the past—the ministry of Jesus and the origin of the church—which event is understood as God's eschatological act; moreover, the documents which this event produced—the New Testament—are apprehended as authoritative revelation.[3] In addition the present itself is seen as having a reality of its own which ought to be meaningful. It is this combination of normative documents from the past with the potential meaningfulness of the present that makes translation—the hermeneutical task—so urgent. How is the past to be related intelligibly through language to the reality that confronts us in the present? We can thus see why hermeneutic has been called the focal theological problem.[4]

Let us now look more closely at theology's interest in a particular past event. And lest this look to the past be disparaged as irrelevant it might be noticed that the nauseated condition, the disturbed existence, of Sartre's Roquentin was owing at least partially to his severance from the past. Roquentin had a sense neither of his own past nor of an objective past so that life had a certain thinness. There is only the present, and behind things there is nothing. As he contemplated his efforts at writing history, he felt as if his sources were only yellowed pages and that they could not really put him in touch with the past. In this position he can say either that he does not exist or that he does exist in the sense that he is surrounded,

[3] Cf. Gerhard Ebeling, *Word and Faith*, trans. J. W. Leitch (Philadelphia: Fortress Press, 1963), p. 32.
[4] *Ibid.*, p. 27.

penetrated, and suffocated by a kind of objective, alien, un-differentiated existence which is the Nausea and which he is.[5] Since, as Sartre's novel suggests (whether or not Sartre intended it), the loss of a meaningful present is the other side of alienation from the past, let us then turn to theology's concern with the biblical history and texts.

One reason why exegesis should endeavor to interpret the biblical texts accurately is simply because, within limits, it is possible. Once men came to see the time-conditioned character of every event or epoch then it became possible—and therefore obligatory—to view each event in its own character and in its difference and distance from our epoch.[6] As Dilthey[7] asserted, each epoch is centered in itself, and while in Dilthey's view each epoch tends to have values which it makes absolute, he sees history itself as having nothing to say about the validity of these various value claims.[8] For Christian exegesis, however, the biblical events and their written witnesses have a normative value. This fact is another reason why exegesis must seek the original historical meaning of the biblical texts. Contemporary interpretations in terms of our own reality must rest on the original meaning.[9] Historical exegesis in its drive for one meaning, the original one, may at first appear to restrict contemporary interpretation,[10] for the allusions in the text which were meaningful to the first hearers may not strike us with any force;[11] but historical accuracy is necessary if the texts are to be able to judge our efforts at translation and are not to be mere sounding boards for our previously held ideas.

[5] Jean Paul Sartre, *Nausea*, trans. L. Alexander (Norfolk, Conn.: New Directions Books, 1959), pp. 31, 130–132, 135, 165, 170–173.

[6] Ebeling, *Word and Faith*, p. 46.

[7] *Pattern*, p. 82.

[8] *Ibid.*, p. 165.

[9] C. H. Dodd, *The Parables of the Kingdom*, p. 157; James D. Smart, *The Interpretation of Scripture*, pp. 37–38.

[10] Ernst Fuchs, *Studies of the Historical Jesus*, p. 87.

[11] Eta Linnemann, *Die Gleichnisse Jesu*, p. 40.

Krister Stendahl in a helpful discussion has posed the hermeneutical problem in terms of "what it meant" and "what it means." A contemporary interpretation of what a text means is to be tested by its faithfulness in rendering the text's original intention, what it meant.[12] While recognizing the validity of

[12] Krister Stendahl, "Biblical Theology, Contemporary," in *The Interpreter's Dictionary of the Bible*, Vol. 1 (New York and Nashville: Abingdon Press, 1962), pp. 421b, 422a, 427a. There appears to be a tacit inconsistency in Stendahl's discussion of the relative merits of Cullmann's and Bultmann's achievements. According to Stendahl, Cullmann is right in identifying time and history as the categories with which the New Testament itself is concerned, and Bultmann is wrong in his concentration on the existential and anthropological (*ibid.*, pp. 421a, 421b, 428a). Stendahl then goes on to say that Bultmann's translation of the New Testament texts into what it means "may" still be valid, but that that would depend on the validity of his hermeneutical principles (*ibid.*, p. 421b). But how could Bultmann's hermeneutical principles make his existentialist translation even possibly valid on Stendahl's terms when Stendahl has asserted that the New Testament is concerned with history, that this concern is antithetical to an existential concern, and that a translation is to be judged by how successfully it communicates the text's original intention?

In the article cited above, Stendahl allowed biblical theology a modest normative function; it has some right to pass judgment—even if tentative—upon the hermeneutical translations made by systematic theology ("Biblical Theology," p. 427a). In a more recent article, however, he seems to deny any normative function to biblical theology, both on methodological grounds and on the ground that the biblical scholar is usually lacking in theological and philosophical knowledge (Krister Stendahl, "Method in the Study of Biblical Theology," in *The Bible in Modern Scholarship*, ed. J. P. Hyatt [New York and Nashville: Abingdon Press, 1965], pp. 199, 202, 204–205). Biblical theology is properly descriptive ("what it meant"), and it is only systematic theology which can deal adequately with the normative question "what it means" ("Method," pp. 199, 202). Stendahl maintains that all Christian theology is biblical in intention, but he assigns to systematic theology the task of deciding whether it has properly translated the biblical intention, of assessing the relationship of the Bible to theology ("Method," pp. 204–205).

In my judgment this position leaves biblical theology unnaturally restricted and its relationship to systematic theology non-existent or unclarified. Stendahl does see biblical theology as a kind of suggestive and creative agitator of the contemporary church and its theology ("Method," pp. 206–208), but just *how* it can be this within his scheme is quite obscure. Moreover, if the biblical theologian does not have the theological and philosophical knowledge to deal with "what it means," the systematic theologian does not have the historical and linguistic tools to know "what it meant." How, then, can he assess the adequacy of his translation and the relationship of his theology to the Bible? The systematic theologian—to follow out Stendahl's logic—will

Stendahl's call for the highest degree of accuracy at the descriptive level of spelling out what the New Testament meant in its own terms,[13] one may retain a certain reserve as to *how* accurate the interpreter can be. We can go a long way in distinguishing the character and thought categories of the many historical epochs, but no interpreter can completely overcome the gap between himself and his text and understand it exactly as did the author or the original audience; therefore, our statement of what the text *meant* is to some degree an interpretation of what it *means*.[14] The exegete simply has to live with the fact that he is never absolutely certain of exactly how wide the gap is between his text and his own view of things or between his text and his exposition. It may be said here by anticipation that precisely because the parables have an aesthetic nature and function, the gap between the hearing of the first audience and the hearing of later interpreters is likely to be smaller than is the case with other kinds of texts.

The possibility of translating the original intention of biblical texts into terms which are meaningful in the present depends on identifying a translatable element in the texts, but before turning to that problem we must give further attention to the need for reconstructing the translatable element in new and altered terminology. That which is obscure in the ancient text must be put into new language which makes the subject matter clear. Such translation, on the one hand, does honor to what the text *meant* historically, for only when its content enters into our familiar language can its original meaning come

simply have to depend on the biblical theologian's view of "what it meant," and he may feel that this leaves him on shaky ground.

Stendahl's exegetical practice in a recent monograph seems more in line with his position in "Biblical Theology" than with his position in "Method." Cf. Krister Stendahl, *The Bible and the Role of Women*, trans. E. T. Sander ("Facet Books—Biblical Series," 15; Philadelphia: Fortress Press, 1966).

[13]Stendahl, "Biblical Theology," pp. 421b–422a.

[14] Cf. Ebeling, *Word and Faith*, pp. 26, 251; James M. Robinson, *The New Hermeneutic*, pp. 74–75.

alive again. The latter may not normally be brought about simply by reciting the text. Translation also honors the present, for only when the text has been interpreted into our language does it enter into our particular world and become really understood.[15] It might be noted that the pre-critical allegorizer also believed that his text had meaning for the present as well as for the past.[16] But instead of recognizing the gap between the text and his own epoch and attempting to make a translation, he simply used the text as a vehicle for his own views.

Ebeling has pointed out that much of our preaching is not understandable because it presupposes faith. Faith is made a prerequisite for hearing with the result that the church's proclamation is a foreign language to the non-believer and may silence the genuine faith of a believer who repudiates religious talk that does not deal with man as he really is. Ebeling is, therefore, inclined to be friendly toward Bonhoeffer's call for a non-religious interpretation of Christianity.[17] In this frame of reference we may note that the parables as told by Jesus did not presuppose faith on the part of his audience; moreover, the lack of specifically religious terminology in the parables might make them especially usable by and suggestive for a non-religious interpretation of Christianity.

Let us now shift our focus of attention slightly from the exegete's obligation to translate the subject matter of his text into contemporary terms to the inevitability of translation. This inevitability was mentioned above primarily as an admission of the interpreter's incapacity to leap over the expanse of time and to get completely inside the mind of an earlier

[15] Ebeling, "Word of God," p. 107; Ebeling, *Word and Faith*, p. 124; Robinson, *New Hermeneutic*, pp. 6–7; Fuchs, *Historical Jesus*, pp. 191, 194, 203–204. See now also Ebeling, *The Problem of Historicity*, trans. Grover Foley (Philadelphia: Fortress Press, 1967), p. 26.
[16] R. M. Grant, *The Letter and the Spirit*, p. 105.
[17] Ebeling, *Word and Faith*, pp. 124–126.

31

author. But this inevitability may also be positively viewed. According to Elizabeth Sewell the fact that we *will* read into older texts more than the author can be supposed to have put there is justified because it is the nature of mind and language together that they form an instrument capable of an indefinite number of developments. Language in general surpasses the writer's powers of exegesis; thus it matters little whether the original author saw the full implication of his work.[18] The biblical exegete may welcome this natural tendency of mind and language to generate new meanings as long as it does not become allegorizing. When it does, the exegete must recall his commitment to the normative particularity of his text. But the language of the text itself may contain meanings that the author was not consciously aware of; and especially in the aesthetic use of language—hence in the parables—does the language itself empower the author to say more than he knows (cf. pp. 75, 77). Therefore, in interpreting the parables for contemporary understanding the texts offer possibilities for translation that are not altogether dependent on the conscious awareness of the author and the original audience.

The position of the new (post-Bultmannian) hermeneutic that biblical texts must be translated into our historically conditioned language if they are to be understood[19] is to be accepted as far as it is appropriate. However, in connection with the parables, two qualifications must be made: (a) Because the parables are aesthetic in nature, they are not as time-conditioned as other biblical texts, and the need for translation is not, therefore, as compelling. (b) Because the parables are aesthetic in nature, it is impossible to translate them completely into any other terms. Linguistic aesthetic objects can be interpreted—translated—to some degree, and the need for

---

[18] Elizabeth Sewell, *The Orphic Voice* (New Haven: Yale University Press, 1960), p. 22.
[19] Robinson, *New Hermeneutic*, p. 7.

clarity justifies the effort, but concomitant with the gain in clarity is a loss in the power of the peculiarly aesthetic function. Therefore, the interpretive translation should explicitly take into account the untranslatable dimension of the parables in order to make the loss as small as possible. The fact that the parables are not completely translatable by us does not contradict my earlier point that the gap between the first- and twentieth-century hearers of the parables is smaller than is the case with other kinds of texts, for the first-century hearers were no more able to translate them completely into other terms than we are.

It is interesting that the theologians associated with the new hermeneutic and its emphasis on the need for translation take the view that when language is operating properly interpretation or translation is unnecessary. The new hermeneutic distinguishes itself from the older hermeneutics of Bultmann and Jonas, which, it is said,[20] understood language as having an inherent tendency to distort the understanding of existence which is seeking to come to expression in it; that is, language objectifies—represents as external and observable—that which is not really able to be made observable. For example, the eschatological becomes an external history of last things rather than, presumably, a crisis and movement in the historical existence of the individual.[21] For the new hermeneutic, however,

[20] Cf. Robinson, *New Hermeneutic*, pp. 32–38.

[21] Cf. Bultmann, "Man between the Times According to the New Testament," in *Existence and Faith*, trans. S. M. Ogden (New York: Meridian Books, 1960), pp. 248–266. It may be, however, that Bultmann held, or came to hold, that it is mythological language rather than language itself which objectifies the subjective, for he sometimes speaks approvingly of analogical language as contrasted with mythological language. God is not spoken of mythologically or even symbolically when his action upon me is seen as an analogue of human relationships and encounters (Bultmann, *Jesus Christ and Mythology* [New York: Scribner's, 1958], pp. 67–69). Yet it is probably true that, for Jonas, language, while inescapable, is also uncongenial to the human spirit's effort to understand itself (cf. Robinson, *New Hermeneutic*, pp. 36–37).

it is language itself which brings the obscure to clarity, the important question being, not what the author intended subjectively to say, but what makes itself visible in the text.[22] According to Ebeling the proper view is not that we need to get an understanding *of* language but that understanding comes *through* language; language brings something to understanding. When a verbal statement operates normally, it is not something obscure which needs the light of understanding from another source. Rather the situation into which the statement is made is obscure and is illumined or brought to understanding by the statement.[23] Similarly, but from a different angle, Fuchs holds that the natural context for the proper functioning of language is the home, where understanding is present; thus language not only mediates understanding but arises from a situation where there is understanding. In the home, people speak, not in order to understand, but because they understand and especially to indicate "what it is time for." The result of Jesus' language was that full clarity prevailed among his hearers.[24]

Fuchs[25] recognizes, however, that the familiar home context which permits language to function properly may disappear and Ebeling,[26] that the mythical does appear in the Bible and needs to be demythologized. Are these only abnormal situations? Ebeling holds that interpretation—hermeneutical aid— is necessary only when the word is hindered from performing its own hermeneutical function, that is, mediating understanding. And that aid consists only in removing the hindrances in order that the word might perform its hermeneutical function. Removing the hindrances evidently means illumining the ob-

[22] Robinson, *New Hermeneutic*, pp. 2, 3, 6, 39, 46.
[23] Ebeling, "Word of God," pp. 93–94.
[24] Ernst Fuchs, "The New Testament and the Hermeneutical Problem," *New Hermeneutic*, pp. 124–126; *Historical Jesus*, p. 74.
[25] "Hermeneutical Problem," p. 126.
[26] "Word of God," p. 100.

scure situation in order that the clear word might be understood, for in Ebeling's view it is the situation and not the word which is the hindrance to understanding.[27] But his position that it is one and not the other seems excessively exclusive. If I do not understand a text because my own confused self-understanding does not permit me to grasp the pattern of connections in the text, the text is still not understandable to me. And if a second word is used to clarify my situation so that I can understand the first word, then the first word is also being illumined; and the fact remains that the first word by itself was not able to clarify my situation. We may agree with Ebeling that understanding finally came from a word and that we do not escape the linguistic realm to attain understanding,[28] but his basic position, that language normally mediates understanding, appears to be an abstraction from the fact that language is always used and heard by people whose understanding of their situation is to some degree clouded.

It would seem that one should say that language sometimes illumines and sometimes obscures, that all linguistic forms do not have the same kind of relationship to their subject matter, and that when language clarifies a situation it also clarifies other language. This is tacitly conceded by Fuchs when he recognizes that the familiar home situation does not always obtain and by Ebeling when he notes that demythologizing is sometimes necessary. There is no reason to think that the situation into which Jesus spoke was particularly abnormal, and the Gospels clearly recognize that Jesus' words, despite their power, did not always bring the situation to clarity: his hearers did not discern the significance of their time (Luke 12:54-57).

Erich Auerbach points to two different ways in which language may function—either of which may be considered normal—in his illuminating contrast of a scene from the

---

[27] *Ibid.*, p. 94.
[28] *Ibid.*

Odyssey with the story of Abraham's near sacrifice of Isaac. In the Greek story men, things, feelings, and thoughts are clearly outlined and brightly illuminated. Everything is externalized and nothing is left in half darkness; Homer knows no background but only a uniformly illuminated foreground. In the Abraham story, on the other hand, we are told nothing about where God came from and nothing about his form or the reason for the command. With regard to the human characters only so much is told as is necessary for the narration, and direct speech serves "to indicate thoughts which remain unexpressed." Very little is externalized and the rest is left in obscurity. "Time and place are undefined and call for interpretation." The whole story is permeated with suspense, remains mysterious, and is "fraught with background."[29] This analysis of an Old Testament story may not be finally incompatible with the view that the proper hermeneutical question is not what lies behind the text but what shows itself in it. This question will have to be conceived broadly enough to allow, however, that what shows itself in some texts may be that there is a great deal that cannot be shown; to be made aware of the latter is in itself a clarification of our situation.

That so many of the parables have had inappropriate concluding statements attached to them is not due entirely to the fact that the original *Sitz im Leben* has been lost. The thought content or meaning of a parable is in principle partially hidden and needs to be clarified or interpreted. But it is not hidden in the allegorical sense, for it is in the parable itself and not in the referent. Presenting ideas or an understanding of existence is, however, a subsidiary level of the parable's main function as an aesthetic object. Thus in order to clarify the thought content one must take a relatively non-aesthetic

[29] Erich Auerbach, *Mimesis*, trans. W. Trask (Garden City, N. Y.: Doubleday Anchor Books, 1957), pp. 1–9.

posture toward the parable, which reduces, as we have noted, the power of its strictly aesthetic function. It is because the expression of thought is a subsidiary level in a parable, because ideas are found only implicitly in the configuration of events, images, and encounters, that the parables, on the one hand, need interpretive clarification and, on the other hand, resist complete translation into any other terms.

2. The Translatable Content of the Parables

Jesus' parables, as we shall see, do have a translatable content; and they also bear in a peculiar way the stamp of Jesus' mind and relate to his historical situation. This means that the parables grasp in their special way something of Jesus' ministry and make it available. But again we must notice that it is not primarily the situation which interprets the parables, but rather the parables interpret his situation and are a part of it. We in turn try to interpret Jesus' ministry in the light of his parables and, secondarily and to a lesser extent, the parables in the light of his ministry.

We noticed in chapter 1 that Jesus called on his audiences to hear his parables with understanding and questioned them about their meaning. Since Jesus intended his parables to be understood and since doubtless they sometimes were, we may say that the parables created freedom for the word or evoked faith.[30] But this freedom for the word which is faith is not a kind of undefinable receptivity or openness for any word. It is freedom to grasp the definite content of this particular word.

It has already been suggested that the subject matter or translatable content of the parables is an understanding of existence. The legitimacy of this position would seem to be

---

[30] Cf. Fuchs, *Historical Jesus*, pp. 76, 77, 81–82, 102; "Hermeneutical Problem," pp. 123–124.

denied by those who maintain that the theology of the New Testament is of the essence of history—the factual—and that this history is not a symbol nor an image nor a mythological framework of "temporal existence."[31] If this antithesis between the historical and the existential is valid with reference to the New Testament in general[32]—which I seriously doubt—it certainly does not apply to the parables, which are not factual (unless by accident) but rather are freely-invented stories. And for Dilthey the purpose of studying history itself is to learn what man is, to grasp the range of the possibilities of human existence. Man does not learn about himself from introspection but through history.[33]

It may be urged, however, that the parables, while being imaginative stories, nevertheless reflect Jesus' concrete historical situation and should be interpreted in the light of that situation (cf. pp. 18–21). We have already seen some of the fallacies of this position, but it is true that the parables make allusions to Jesus' *Sitz im Leben*. These allusions, however, are taken up into a new configuration—the parabolic story— and derive their meaning from the latter. Thus they do not give us direct access to the facts of Jesus' ministry. For example, in The Ten Maidens the conduct of the foolish maidens may be an allusion to a certain type of behavior in Jesus' historical situation; but the maidens' behavior receives its meaning from the final issue of the *story*: they are shut out of the wedding feast. Those who behave in a certain way lose the very thing which they seek. The end of the story, however, that is, the *exclusion*, does not refer to anything in Jesus' situation; thus

[31] Oscar Cullmann, "The Necessity and Function of Higher Criticism," in *The Early Church*, trans. A. J. B. Higgins (Philadelphia: Westminster Press, 1956), p. 8.

[32] As Stendahl seems to imply ("Biblical Theology," p. 421a).

[33] Dilthey, *Pattern*, pp. 39, 60, 71–72, 90, 92, 103.

the hearers are made to see their behavior in relation to something not already present in their situation. They are given a new perspective on—a new word about—the latter. This means that the nature of the parables, as well as the inherent probabilities of the case, points to the fact that Jesus was not giving information about his situation but an understanding of the possibilities of existence which his situation brought. If the one-talent man in The Talents points to the Pharisees who "hoard the law," as he speaks in the dialogue he also gives voice to the understanding and state of existence which are exemplified in his own conduct in the parable, or in the Pharisees' hoarding of the law, as well as in innumerable other possible concrete cases; furthermore, this existential self-understanding is taken up into a dramatic configuration which is basically human. It is not necessary, then, to add anything to the parable in order to make it contemporary (and this is true of all of the parables as we have defined the term); all one need do is to translate—as much as is necessary and possible—the understanding of existence which is already in it.

Thus Bultmann's basic hermeneutical principle—that the most adequate question to put to the Bible, as to any significant text, is what its understanding of the possibilities of human existence is[34]—is eminently appropriate for the parables. It may be agreed that the biblical text transcends the author's self-understanding and that our proper concern is an understanding of the subject matter.[35] We noted in the preceding section that especially the author of artistic works says more than he knows he is saying. At the same time his work does not completely transcend his self-understanding; and the subject matter may be held to be an understanding of existence, even if it is too restrictive of the possibilities of meaning in the

[34] Bultmann, "Hermeneutics," pp. 235, 246, 253; *Jesus Christ*, pp. 52–53.
[35] Cf. Robinson, *New Hermeneutic*, p. 77.

text to hold that the subject matter is the author's self-understanding.[36]

The term "existence" as I have been using it—and as it is used in existentialist theology—does not refer to something like the "inner man." It means man in historical encounters in the world, man as an essentially linguistic being using his language to understand his place in history.[37] The parables also suggest this understanding of existence, for they dramatize man's existential possibilities through concrete historical encounters, and the linguistic factor is seen both in Jesus' telling of the parables and in the importance of dialogue within them.

---

[36] The view that the translatable content of the parables is their understanding of existence and that this is still relevant for us presupposes that there is through the ages a certain persistence of the essentials of human existence, a continuity of general human nature or of things held in common (Linnemann, *Gleichnisse*, p. 40; Dilthey, *Pattern*, pp. 67–68, 77–78, 111–112, 120, 123). It is also true that each epoch is historically individuated, that the gulf in time between text and author cannot be completely spanned, and that the essentials of existence must repeatedly find new expression (cf. Robinson, *New Hermeneutic*, pp. 59, 72–75; Robert W. Funk, "The Hermeneutical Problem and Historical Criticism," *New Hermeneutic*, pp. 189–190; Linnemann, *Gleichnisse*, p. 40). Thus we have to do with translation and not with becoming contemporary with the author and reliving his experiences (Robinson, *New Hermeneutic*, p. 59). Dilthey went too far in affirming the sameness of mind in author and interpreter (Dilthey, *Pattern*, pp. 67–68). Yet he did recognize that there are differences between individuals and their expressions of life and that it is just these differences that make interpretation necessary (pp. 77, 111–112, 136–137). Dilthey affirms that the differences between individuals are a matter of degree and are not qualitative (pp. 111–112), which seems to be what the logic of his position calls for. However, he also at times seems to speak of individuality as qualitative (pp. 136–137). Dilthey must certainly be right that interpretation would be impossible if expressions of life were completely strange (p. 77).

[37] Cf. Bultmann, "Hermeneutics," p. 260; James M. Robinson, "The Formal Structure of Jesus' Message," in *Current Issues in New Testament Interpretation*, ed. W. Klassen and G. F. Snyder (New York: Harper, 1962), pp. 93–94; Robinson, *New Hermeneutic*, pp. 47–48; Ebeling, "Word of God," p. 104; Fuchs, *Historical Jesus*, pp. 89, 211; Heinrich Ott, "The Historical Jesus and the Ontology of History," in *The Historical Jesus and the Kerygmatic Christ*, trans. and ed. C. E. Braaten and R. A. Harrisville (New York and Nashville: Abingdon Press, 1964), p. 145.

Action and talk are interwoven so that the meaning of the former comes to expression in the latter.

A parable as a whole dramatizes an ontological possibility—that which is there and possible in principle for man as man—and the two basic ontological (human) possibilities which the parables present are the gain or loss of existence, becoming authentic or inauthentic. The prodigal son gains his existence, and the unforgiving servant loses his. But each parable also depicts how existence is ontically[38]—actually and concretely—gained or lost, and the aesthetic form presses the two—the ontological and the ontic—into a unity. We could then say that each parable dramatizes how the basic human possibilities of gaining or losing existence may actually occur. The ontological and the ontic—the what and how of the possibilities of ex-

---

[38] According to Bultmann, theology must show that its view of the ontic is consistent with philosophy's analysis of what is ontologically possible if the man of faith is not to be removed from humanity. And theology is dependent on philosophy for this analysis (Bultmann, "The Historicity of Man and Faith," in *Existence and Faith*, pp. 94–99; "Hermeneutics," p. 258). But can the ontological and the ontic be so neatly separated and can theology simply concede this dependence on philosophy (not that there should be no dialogue)? One wonders whether philosophy is as free from ontic implications as Bultmann ("Historicity," pp. 95–96; *Jesus Christ*, pp. 55–59) sometimes suggests and also whether theology can disavow ontological reflections of its own. Bultmann ("Historicity," p. 101) allows that ontic experience may enrich ontological understanding and that the New Testament does contain ontological reflections, though its main concern is ontic (Bultmann, *Theology of the New Testament*, Vol. 1, trans. K. Grobel [New York: Scribner's, 1951], pp. 198–199, 209–210, 212, 227–228). If the ontic must be ontologically possible, is it not likely that the ontological implications of the New Testament's ontic views will conflict with the ontology of any given philosophy? For Bultmann, faith, for example, is an ontological possibility (Bultmann, "Historicity," pp. 96, 108), but it is ontically—actually—impossible for sinful man on his own and is ontically possible only as response to the grace of the proclaimed word (Bultmann, *Theology*, Vol. 1, p. 269; "New Testament and Mythology," in *Kerygma and Myth*, Vol. 1, trans. R. H. Fuller [London: S.P.C.K., 1954], pp. 22–33). Thus we see from some statements of Bultmann himself that the ontological is of relevance only in connection with the ontic.

istence—are integrated in one configuration of action and in-terpretation.

The ontic element—how existence is lost or gained—may be analogous to something in Jesus' situation, as the prodigal's behavior is in some way analogous to that of the publicans and sinners. The mistake of the rigorously historical approach is to isolate this element and interpret it in the light of Jesus' historical situation instead of as an organic part of an under-standing of existence which is implicitly present in the story as a whole. Hence the aesthetic unity of the parable is broken and its most enduring subject matter—its most appropriate content for translation—is lost sight of.

The existential approach does more justice to the non-allegorical nature of the parables and to the general absence of specifically religious terminology in them than does an ap-proach which speaks of them as embodying the moral insight and religious experience of their creator. T. W. Manson, who uses the latter terminology, also speaks of the moral-religious element as a "further" meaning which is in addition to the story meaning. Manson argues that David was able to see the story meaning of Nathan's Ewe Lamb (II Sam. 12:1-4) but not the further meaning of its application to himself—until it was pointed out to him. Manson, however, overcomes some-what this dichotomy as his discussion progresses.[39] The ex-istential approach need not speak of a further meaning be-cause there is one (translatable) meaning, namely, the pattern of connections in the story. It might also be pointed out that Nathan's Ewe Lamb is closer to an example story than to a parable. In addition to the foregoing, it may be suggested that existential interpretation is inherently more productive than other approaches often are. A. M. Hunter, who gives allegiance to the historical method, recognizes the eschatological crisis

[39] T. W. Manson, *The Teaching of Jesus*, pp. 80–81, 65–66, 70–73.

note of Jesus' teaching, but in his effort to make the parables contemporary he turns to "moralizing." Thus his exposition of The Talents becomes an exhortation to use one's talents in everyday living[40] instead of an analysis of the crisis of the loss of existence.

Whether the existential approach is justified will finally depend on the exegetical fruits which it yields, and here we are involved in the circular thinking that always attends the attempt to clarify presuppositions. Asking the existential question enables one to see certain things in the parables, and what is seen will have to be the criterion of whether this is the right question.

3. How the Translation Is Accomplished

In order to translate the subject matter of a text into our terms it is obviously necessary to grasp the meaning of the text itself. Dilthey's view of how history is understood is quite applicable—though with exceptions—to the parables, or to other prose fiction or drama. Meaning resides in intelligible patterns of connections and relationships, and understanding is grasping these connections, that is, grasping the meaning.[41] Thus the first step is to comprehend the pattern of connections in the parables themselves. The nature of these connections in artistic prose will have to be considered more carefully in chapter 3.

The second step is the translation itself. Fuchs states that the correct hermeneutical principle calls for connecting the form (the external language) of the text with the content in

[40] A. M. Hunter, *Interpreting the Parables*, pp. 39, 99, 106–108.

[41] Dilthey, *Pattern*, pp. 73–75, 89, 99–100, 106. The view of typological exegesis held by Lampe and Woollcombe is very close to Dilthey's view of understanding history. Typological exegesis is not the search for hidden meanings underlying the obvious one but the making explicit of real correspondences, links, or connections between the various events of salvation history; cf. G. W. H. Lampe and K. J. Woollcombe, *Essays on Typology* ("Studies in Biblical Theology," No. 22 [London: SCM Press, 1957]), pp. 29, 39, 40, 68.

order that the life of the text can appear. This does not mean giving new life to the form but letting the life or content be expressed in the form of our language.[42] Fuch's point seems to suggest a separation of form and content which is not possible with language used aesthetically. The form—or shape or linguistic connections—is not just a container for the content; rather, the meaning is in the form-and-content. That is why linguistic aesthetic objects cannot be completely translated: to give a new form changes the meaning. To the extent that a parable can be translated, however, Fuchs is right that the meaning must be given a new form or pattern of connections. This form will express what the text's content can do in our situation.[43] The meaning distilled from the form-and-content must be given a new form-and-content, a new pattern of connections which relates the original meaning to our time. But since the interpretation of a parable—as distinguished from the parable itself—is not an aesthetic object, the relationship of form to content in the interpretation will not be the same as it is in the parable.

We must keep in mind that meaning does not reside merely in pivotal words or concepts but also in the chain or pattern of connections. As Laeuchli has pointed out, unless one is aware of this, he may think that he is giving a translation of the original meaning while not doing so at all. The exegete must constantly be aware of the tension between the form of the biblical language and the new form of his translation.[44]

How then is one enabled to see the pattern of connections in a text? According to Dilthey the basis of understanding others and texts about them is our own experience. By reflecting on the pattern of connections within our own interior lives we

---

[42] Fuchs, *Historical Jesus*, p. 194.
[43] *Ibid.*, p. 204.
[44] Samuel Laeuchli, *The Language of Faith* (New York and Nashville: Abingdon Press, 1962), pp. 16, 47, 91–93, 183.

are able to see the interconnections of other complexes. Understanding passes from something already grasped to something
new which can be understood through it.[45] Building on this
foundation Bultmann has developed his concept of pre-understanding. One cannot understand a text unless particular questions are asked of it, and these questions are prompted and
informed by the relationship to and understanding of the subject matter of the text which the interpreter already has. Thus
understanding depends on a pre-understanding of the subject
matter.[46] It should be recognized that pre-understanding is not
just a matter of psychological inwardness but includes one's
awareness of belonging to historical communities and also includes the language in which the communal relationships take
shape.[47] In fact it may be doubted whether thought—or any
very significant thought—can take place at all without language.[48]

This basic insight that pre-understanding is necessary for
the acquirement of understanding has considerable biblical support. In Proverbs 9:7-9 the wise are capable of becoming wiser,

[45] Dilthey, *Pattern*, pp. 39, 66, 86–87, 94, 107, 116, 140.

[46] Bultmann, "Hermeneutics," pp. 239–243; *Jesus Christ*, pp. 46–50.

[47] Dilthey has been criticized for conceiving of pre-understanding too inwardly and subjectively (cf. Robinson, *New Hermeneutic*, pp. 69–70) and
Bultmann, for doing less than full justice to the historical conditionedness
of pre-understanding (Funk, "The Hermeneutical Problem," pp. 188–191).
According to Gadamer we understand ourselves first as part of a family, society, and state; and these historic relationships transcend the experiential
horizon of the individual and take shape primarily in our language (cf. Robinson, *New Hermeneutic*, pp. 69–70). While this criticism is probably essentially justified, it should be noted that Dilthey and Bultmann do not ignore
completely man's position in larger communal structures (Dilthey, *Pattern*,
pp. 94, 140; Bultmann, "Hermeneutics," pp. 255, 259–260); moreover, despite the animus of much contemporary theology toward anything psychological, psychological inwardness is still a part of pre-understanding.

[48] Philip Wheelwright, *Metaphor and Reality* (Bloomington: Indiana
University, 1962), pp. 19–20, 128; Frederick Ferré, *Language, Logic, and
God* (New York: Harper, 1961), pp. 37, 157; Paul Van Buren, "On Doing
Theology" (unpublished paper from Drew Consultation on Hermeneutic,
April, 1964), p. 2; Ernst Fuchs, *Hermeneutik* (Bad Cannstatt: R. Müller-
schön, 1958), p. 131.

but the foolish are hopeless; the same principle appears with some frequency in the rabbinic literature (Aboth 1:13; Berachoth 40a).[49] In the Synoptic Gospels the thought is rather prominent that he who has will receive more while he who has not will lose what he has. Matthew (or his source) applies this saying externally and superficially to The Talents (25:29); the ten-talent man receives the talent taken from the one-talent man. And in 13:12 the "more" which the disciples will receive seems to refer to the special privilege of private explanations of the parables by Jesus (cf. Matt. 13:10, 18, 36). But in Mark 4:25 and Luke 8:18 the point is that those who hear with understanding will acquire more understanding.

We have adopted the view that the translatable content of the parables is an understanding of existence. Furthermore, because they are associated by Jesus in some way with the kingdom of God while the evangelists associate them with their kerygmatic interest, we must say that the parables are concerned with existence in faith. Is it then necessary for the pre-understanding which can understand the parables—or any biblical text—to include adherence to the Christian faith?

It has been held that faith is necessary in order to understand the Scriptures in general[50] or the historical Jesus in particular.[51] Or more particularly it has been affirmed that we believe in the urgency of the parables "because they were spoken by a particular person with a special status."[52] That would mean that we would have to believe in Jesus as the Christ before we could take the parables seriously.

Bultmann also has been accused of assuming that one must

[49] W. O. E. Oesterley, *The Gospel Parables in the Light of Their Jewish Background*, pp. 55–56.

[50] Smart, *Interpretation*, p. 30.

[51] J. Arthur Baird, *The Justice of God in the Teaching of Jesus*, pp. 20–21; Hugh Anderson, *Jesus and Christian Origins* (New York: Oxford University Press, 1964), pp. 83–85.

[52] Geraint V. Jones, *The Art and Truth of the Parables*, p. 160.

become a believer in order to understand,[53] but he has explicitly denied that one must have faith in order to understand the conceptual themes of the Christian faith.[54] It is true that the faith of the evangelists shaped the Gospels and also undoubtedly affected their understanding of the parables, but as far as Jesus' own situation was concerned, his words were not heard as divinely authenticated revelations but as the human words of the carpenter from Nazareth.[55] And the unbeliever who hears them today need not accept them as authoritative before he understands them.

If Bultmann is right that faith is not necessary for understanding the subject matter of biblical texts, he is also right that one must, nevertheless, be stirred by questions about his own existence. The texts speak only to those who are concerned about the kind of question to which faith is a possible answer.[56] To understand the parables, to grasp the pattern of connections in them, it is then necessary to have the pre-understanding that existence can be gained or lost, that there is a definable difference between authenticity and inauthenticity.

It has already been implied and needs to be stated clearly

[53] Amos N. Wilder, "New Testament Hermeneutics Today," in *Current Issues in New Testament Interpretation*, p. 41.

[54] Rudolf Bultmann, "Historicity," p. 101; "The Case for Demythologizing," in *Kerygma and Myth*, Vol. 2, trans. R. H. Fuller (London: S.P.C.K., 1962), p. 187. Fuchs is in essential agreement with Bultmann (*Historical Jesus*, pp. 184, 186).

[55] Linnémann, *Gleichnisse*, pp. 42–43. When Hugh Anderson suggests that in a proper hermeneutic the faith of the interpreter should have a key place in knowing and describing historical reality (*Jesus*, p. 84), he seems to be confusing the role of faith in salvation and the role of faith in theological interpretation. Or to put it from a slightly different angle, the role of faith in writing the Gospels is confused with its role in interpreting them. An accurate interpreter of the Gospels will recognize that the resurrection faith is central in them (Anderson, *Jesus*, p. 84), but that does not mean that the interpreter must have faith in order to recognize the prominence and nature of the evangelists' faith. In short, Anderson has not sufficiently distinguished faith and theology.

[56] Bultmann, "Hermeneutics," p. 256; "Case," p. 187; "Is Exegesis without Presuppositions Possible?" in *Existence and Faith*, p. 294.

that a pre-understanding influences what the interpreter sees in his text, for an interpretation incorporates the prior understanding that grows out of the interpreter's own experience.[57] And if, as we have seen, language is a part of our pre-understanding, then our language conditions the fact that, and the manner in which, reality confronts us.[58] Wheelwright has argued forcefully that the language which we have inherited both makes possible and limits the questions we can ask, the kinds of reality we can conceive, and the ways we can conceive it.[59]

James Barr strongly opposes this viewpoint. On the basis of scientific and comparative linguistic studies he maintains that there is no close relationship between the vocabulary grids and morphological and syntactical structures of a language, on the one hand, and the thought structure and apprehension of reality of the users of the language, on the other hand. Language is a socially conditioned, arbitrary system of semantic markers. There can be no internal Christian meaning of a word in the New Testament, for example, while it retains its external Greek meaning, because words have no more than their semantic function. In Barr's view the connection between biblical language and biblical thought in its apprehension of reality does not reside in the structure of the language, nor in the new conceptual content given to words by the biblical writers; the connection lies, rather, in the combination of words in sentences, with the value of the words changing little or not at all. The real bearer of thought is the sentence or the larger unit of the speech or poem.[60]

[57] Bultmann, "Hermeneutics," pp. 241–242; Dilthey, *Pattern*, pp. 100, 109.
[58] Ebeling, *Word and Faith*, p. 248; cf. also Amos N. Wilder, *Early Christian Rhetoric*, pp. 13–17.
[59] Wheelwright, *Metaphor*, pp. 24–31; *The Burning Fountain*, p. 6.
[60] James Barr, *The Semantics of Biblical Language* (Oxford: The University Press, 1961), pp. 38–39, 42, 49, 204, 244–245, 263–266.

Barr is probably right that too much theological weight has been rested on linguistic views which will not stand up under scrutiny. However, the biblical *Sitz im Leben* of faith and worship has probably contributed more new conceptual content to certain words, that is, has created more technical terms, than Barr allows for. This is a point which he might have been more attentive to in view of his emphasis on the socially conditioned character of language. Moreover, if word combinations are important in grasping and expressing reality, one should be cognizant of the fact that new and peculiar *combinations* may occur. It might also be pointed out that there is evidence from psychological studies which suggests the influence of the poverty or wealth of one's vocabulary upon one's perception of reality.[61] Finally, there may well be interaction between the apprehension of reality and the larger linguistic units which Barr mentions. It is neither accidental nor inconsequential for the grasp of reality that the basic mode of speech in the Bible is the story[62] rather than, say, the lyric poem.

Before leaving this section, two criticisms of the whole idea of pre-understanding may be mentioned:

(1) Exegesis guided by pre-understanding is lacking in objectivity and can only establish what it already knows. Historical sources are not allowed to say their own word and express their alien subject matter, but rather sources of the greatest variety are all made to speak the same language.[63]

To this criticism it should be said that pre-understanding does not determine in advance what the content of a text will

---

[61] See Andrew T. Weil, "Harvard's Bruner and His Yeasty Ideas," *Harper's*, 229 (December, 1964), 85.

[62] Cf. Wilder, *Rhetoric*, pp. 37–38; Laeuchli, *Language*, p. 232.

[63] Johannes Munck, "The New Testament and Gnosticism," in *Current Issues in New Testament Interpretation*, p. 232. It is not clear why Anderson (*Jesus*, p. 182) is critical of the place of faith and existential openness in the new quest of the historical Jesus when in another context he states that faith should play a part in interpretation (*ibid.*, p. 84).

be but only determines what kind of subject matter will be looked for. Unless interpretation is guided by some question, it will not see anything, except haphazardly; and the most objective exegesis will be that which is guided by a question informed by a pre-understanding of what is actually in the text.[64] It is true that Bultmann[65] makes the value judgment that the most significant question to ask of a biblical text is the existential question, but he does not consider this the only relevant question. Nor does he make all texts say the same thing. He expounds, for example, the different understandings of existence in classical Greek, Stoic, gnostic, and biblical thought.[66]

(2) It seems to be implicit in the position of Heinrich Ott that pre-understanding is unnecessary for understanding. Historical reality overwhelmingly forces and impresses *itself* upon us as a picture or point of view. This interpretation is not created by us, but, rather, reality first impresses itself upon us in the form of pictures.[67] Similarly Ott maintains that man with his ability to speak does not simply invent speech as the opportunity arises. A man could not have written a poem about a wood, for example, had the wood not first spoken to him.[68]

There is some point to Ott's position, for if understanding depended entirely on pre-understanding, we could not come to

[64] Bultmann, "Hermeneutics," pp. 255–256; "Is Exegesis," pp. 293–294.
[65] "Hermeneutics," pp. 247, 253; "Case," p. 185; "Is Exegesis," pp. 293–294.
[66] Bultmann, "The Understanding of Man and the World in the New Testament and in the Greek World," in *Essays Philosophical and Theological*, pp. 67–89.
[67] Ott, "Historical Jesus," pp. 157, 161.
[68] Heinrich Ott, "The Problem of Non-objectifying Thinking and Speaking in Theology" (unpublished paper from Drew Consultation on Hermeneutic, April, 1964), p. 7. Here we see the influence of the later Heidegger, with language, as the house of being, speaking through man rather than man doing the speaking. Cf. James M. Robinson, "The German Discussion of the Later Heidegger," in *The Later Heidegger and Theology*, ed. James M. Robinson and J. B. Cobb, Jr. (New York: Harper, 1963), pp. 44, 49–50.

understand anything that we did not already understand, but the fact is that we do. At birth we understand nothing; thus there must be some points at which historical reality impresses its meaning upon us apart from pre-understanding. Bultmann at least tacitly recognizes this when he says that pre-understanding comes from the way historical phenomena themselves speak to us.[69] This pre-understanding is *pre*-understanding in relation to later understanding, but at the time it is acquired it is an understanding that comes from an encounter with historical existence itself.

It would seem then that in understanding there is continuing mutual interaction between the patterns of meaning in history itself and our pre-understanding. Ott does not sufficiently recognize the reality and critical capacity of pre-understanding. It may be, as Ott claims,[70] that brute facts are only abstractions from the picture or significance-laden character of history itself. But that does not mean, as Ott also claims,[71] that all historical knowledge is through encounter and that there is no such thing as objective historical knowledge. History —and its sources—does not simply overwhelm us. We may agree that history itself has patterns of meaning, but one may recognize differing patterns of meaning in various historical phenomena and also distinguish them from one's own normative frame of reference. But this is not to deny that our pre-understanding does always inject something of "what it means" into our interpretation of "what it meant."

In concluding this section let it be said that in our approach to the parables there is interaction between our pre-understanding which prompts the existential question and our recognition that the parables themselves are concerned with an understanding of existence.

---

[69] Bultmann, "Hermeneutics," p. 255.
[70] "Historical Jesus," p. 157.
[71] *Ibid.*, pp. 145, 147–148, 161.

4. The Goal of Interpretation

The goal of the hermeneutical endeavor, the purpose of translating a biblical text into new terms, is that the language of the text might become an event. It is hoped that the hearer will be brought to see that the cap fits—or does not fit—that the point hits home, that the subject matter concerns him. The word is to become a happening word or language event.[72]

In Jesus' sayings and parables he brought together the presence of God and the context of daily living.[73] That does not mean that the parables give enlightenment about the constitution of the rule of God (even when they begin "The kingdom of heaven is like") but that they portray an existential state and show the listener what he must now do.[74] Jesus' parables were a language event in his day, and the purpose of interpreting them is that that event might occur once more in the exposition.

From the standpoint of linguistic analysis language has several legitimate functions, and one of these is the performative function. Language when exercising this function *does* something—declares war or opens a highway.[75] It is because the performative is one of the possible functions of language that

[72] Ebeling, *Word and Faith*, p. 124; Fuchs, *Historical Jesus*, pp. 79, 86–87, 196. Ebeling's suggestion ("Word of God," p. 103) that the event character of the biblical word is supported by the meaning of the Hebrew word *dabar* is questionable. As Barr has pointed out (*Semantics*, pp. 131–132) it may be a part of Old Testament theology that the word of God enters history as a dynamic event, but that does not mean that "event" is any part of the meaning of the word *dabar*.

[73] Fuchs, "Hermeneutical Problem," pp. 129–130.

[74] Fuchs, *Historical Jesus*, pp. 86, 140; Linnemann, *Gleichnisse*, p. 31.

[75] Ferré, *Language*, pp. 55–56. Apparently it was J. L. Austin who first used the term "performative" to designate a certain class of utterances: utterances which are not nonsense and yet are not true or false. One who makes such an utterance does, rather than merely says, something. He apologizes, bets, promises, names, or marries (*Philosophical Papers*, ed. J. O. Urmson and G. J. Warnock [Oxford: The Clarendon Press, 1962], pp. 222 ff.). Austin probably used the term performative function in a more specific sense than I have. At the same time he does include imperatives and warnings

language can become an event. We noted earlier that there are differences of function between the parable as aesthetic and its interpretation as non-aesthetic, but that does not mean that both of them may not be included in the category of the language event. They execute different aspects of the performative function, but they both have the same goal, which is to involve the hearer in the subject matter. Thus what is said about the nature of the parables as a language event also applies essentially to a proper interpretation of them.

(1) Jesus' parables were a language event in that they injected a new possibility into the situation of his hearers. The latter were offered a new way of understanding their situation in history.[76] If historical being inherently includes an understanding of existence, a grasp of the pattern of connections, then giving a new understanding does introduce a real, new possibility; the situation is changed.

(2) The parables were a language event because they called for a judgment from the hearers. They were asked not merely to see the understanding of existence in a parable but to assent to it.[77] Jeremias has pointed out that especially the formula *tis ex humōn* ("who among you") (Matt. 6:27 and Luke 12:25; Matt. 7:9 and Luke 11:11; Matt. 12:11 and Luke 14:5; Luke 11:5; 14:28; 15:4; 17:7) by its direct address seeks to force the hearer to accept a definite position. This formula seems to have no contemporary parallels, though it occurs in the prophets (Isa. 42:23; 50:10; Hag. 2:3) but not as the introduction to a parable.[78] It is probably not accidental, however, that this in-

---

among performative utterances (*Philosophical Papers*, pp. 230–231), and Jesus' parables, as well as the theological interpretation of them, are at least implicit calls to decision.

[76] Linnemann, *Gleichnisse*, pp. 33, 38.

[77] Linnemann, *Gleichnisse*, pp. 25, 27–28; Oesterley, *Parables*, p. 5; A. T. Cadoux, *The Parables of Jesus*, p. 45; Dodd, *Parables*, pp. 11–12; Hunter, *Parables*, p. 12; Nils A. Dahl, "The Parables of Growth," p. 138.

[78] Joachim Jeremias, *The Parables of Jesus*, p. 103.

terrogative formula does not appear with any of the fully developed narrative parables. In the case of the latter the story itself does the work, and the call for a judgment is indirect.

The judgment which is evoked by the parables entails a far-reaching decision, for the pre-understanding of the hearers is challenged, and they must decide between their old understanding and the new one that confronts them in the parable.[79] While Jesus' parables placed the hearers inescapably in the situation of decision, Jesus could not determine how people would decide. Those who refused his word made a decision and were hardened in their old existence. Those who accepted his new understanding were carried across the disunity of decision and challenge and into a new situation of unity and adjustment.[80]

In Linnemann's view the decision is evoked by the narrator's making clear the conflict between himself and his audience. The hearers must clearly recognize the correspondence between the image part (the parable story) and the material part (in the sense of Jesus' historical situation) in order that they might take up the same attitude toward the image part which they have toward the corresponding aspects of the material part. The narrator accomplishes this by giving room in the parable to the audience's judgment on the situation, but with this he interlaces his own judgment, to which he hopes to win them.[81]

We may question whether Jesus' hearers could have been and needed to be as clearly aware of the correspondences between the parable and the situation, as Linnemann holds. Because the parable is a cohesive unity, its points of contact with the historical situation are fused into the new pattern of con-

---

[79] Cf. Fuchs, *Historical Jesus*, p. 221; Linnemann, *Gleichnisse*, pp. 30, 38.
[80] Cf. Fuchs, *Historical Jesus*, pp. 221–222.
[81] Linnemann, *Gleichnisse*, pp. 34–35.

nections which the parable is so that the awareness of correspondence with the historical situation would be at a lower level of consciousness than Linnemann seems to allow. The hearers of The Unjust Steward, say, would hardly have had their attention drawn immediately to the impending apocalyptic dissolution of the world which Jesus proclaimed in his non-parabolic teaching. Moreover, Linnemann's analysis has the hearer's judgment move from his knowledge of his situation to the parable rather than from the parable to a new understanding of his situation; and thus the power of the parable to be a new word is vitiated. In any case, we need not know what the original audience's pre-understanding was in order to give a satisfactory contemporary interpretation of the parables,[82] because a parable's understanding of existence is primarily *in* its *own* pattern of connections, in its form-and-content. The theological interpretation of the parables evokes a decision from us when it juxtaposes a translated view of the parable's existential understanding with contemporary self-understandings or with a translation of the Bible's view of sinful man's self-understanding. Thus theological reflection, as well as the original texts, may be a language event because it conducts man to a place[83]—the place of decision. Theology does not do this, how-

---

[82] As Linnemann claims (*Gleichnisse*, pp. 30–31).

[83] Ott, "Non-objectifying Thinking," p. 19. The way German theology has sometimes been described as arriving at the concept of a language event (cf. Robinson, *New Hermeneutic*, p. 57) might lead one to suppose that the concept was first discovered by contemporary German theologians. It should be pointed out that the concept, if not the term, was briefly and clearly delineated by Dodd (*Parables*, pp. 5, 159) and Manson (*Teaching*, pp. 65–66, 70–73, 81) in their discussions of Jesus' use of parables. According to Manson the parables were not merely illustrations or embellishments of theological ideas but were the word of God itself piercing the self-satisfaction and worldly care of man, arousing his conscience, and capable of carrying him over into faith. I would not question that the exposition of the language character of man's existence and the use of existentialist terminology are an advance. At the same time Dodd's and Manson's discussions are not entirely

ever, by being non-objectifying thought,[84] that is, thought which can avoid using the subject's categories in speaking *about* an object. It does it because clarifying the nature of faith and the issue of decision helps to lead man to decision.[85]

We might also remind ourselves that literary critics speak of language becoming an event[86] and of a poem, novel, or story testing a reader and having the power to move him into a new state of being or into the experience of a new horizon.[87] This does not by any means solve all of the problems of the relationship between Scripture texts and literary art (see chap. 3), but it does suggest that a fruitful rapprochement is possible, which is important in view of the fact that the parables are both biblical texts and works of art.

(3) If the goal of the hermeneutical effort is the language event, then it is not ultimately the text which is interpreted and clarified, but the interpreter and his situation are illuminated. This point has been well made by Fuchs and Ebeling,[88] but how this can be called a step beyond Bultmann and how it can be said that for Bultmann the interpretation of the text is the ultimate goal[89] is incomprehensible to me. It is certainly clear that for Bultmann the word may be an event.[90]

lost on us, and they make us realize that the possibility of language's becoming an event and of our understanding it does not depend on whether that happening should be called a *Sprachereignis*, a *Sprechereignis*, or a *Wortgeschehen*.

[84] As Ott claims ("What is Systematic Theology?" in *Later Heidegger*, pp. 91–93, 106–109).

[85] Bultmann, "Case," p. 183.

[86] Sewell, *Orphic*, p. 23.

[87] Eliseo Vivas, *The Artistic Transaction* (Ohio State University Press, 1963), p. 174; Michael Novak, "Philosophy and Fiction," *The Christian Scholar*, 47 (1964), 101, 108; Tom F. Driver, "The Arts and the Christian Evangel," *The Christian Scholar*, 40 (1957), 335–336.

[88] Fuchs, *Historical Jesus*, pp. 206, 212; Ebeling, "Word of God," pp. 93–96, 109.

[89] Cf. Robinson, *New Hermeneutic*, pp. 52–53.

[90] Bultmann, "Case," pp. 191–193.

Moreover, for him interpretation claims the interpreter, challenges his pre-understanding, requires decision, and has the goal of giving him an understanding of himself.[91]

Even those New Testament scholars—like Fuchs and Linnemann—who have been most concerned to understand the parables as language events have not fully exploited the event character of the parables, for they have not seriously considered how the parables' peculiarly aesthetic function enhances their character as events. This will be one of our concerns in chapter 3.

5. The Parables and the Ultimate Referent of Theological Language

In the previous sections of this chapter we have considered the translatable content of the parables—an understanding of existence—and the relationship of the parables to their audience—as a language event. We have also touched on how they are related to the historical situation in which they arose. We turn now to consider them in relation to their ultimate referent, God, for the existence in history of which they give us an understanding is an existence on which God impinges. The parables refer to God only indirectly, but they still intend in some way to refer to him. Therefore, in examining the parables we are confronted with the question how—and whether—God can be spoken of meaningfully at all. How—and can—assertions be made about God and his actions?

According to the logical positivism represented in Ayer's *Language, Truth, and Logic* if a statement is to have any meaning as a factual statement or assertion, some sense expe-

---

[91] Bultmann, *Jesus and the Word*, trans. L. P. Smith and E. H. Lantero (New York: Scribner Library, 1958), pp. 4, 8, 10; "Hermeneutics," pp. 253–254; *Jesus Christ*, p. 53; "Is Exegesis," pp. 294, 296.

rience must be relevant for its verification.[92] Antony Flew would disclaim being a logical positivist,[93] but the version of the verification principle which he applies against theological statements seems not too far removed from positivism. For a statement to be a meaningful assertion it must also deny something. What it denies is what could count against it or falsify it. If it cannot be falsified, it cannot be verified. If nothing can count against it, it cannot be an assertion.[94]

The application of the verification principle puts statements about God into the category of meaningless nonsense statements.[95] According to Flew religious people will not allow that anything counts against their affirmations: "God loves us" seems to be compatible with *any* state of affairs, however tragic or pitiable. Therefore, statements about God are made to die the death of a thousand qualifications and to become vacuous.[96] Paul Van Buren has vigorously maintained that modern man, who is empirically minded, can make no sense of the term "God" nor of the category of the transcendent.[97]

In criticism of positivism's use of the verification principle it may be pointed out that the principle itself cannot be verified by sense experience but rests instead on a basic conviction or presupposition—that there is no reality beyond that which

[92] This was Ayer's position in the 1935 edition of *Language, Truth, and Logic* (cf. the preface to the 1935 edition on p. 31 of the 1946 edition). However, in the introduction to the 1946 edition he held the word "relevant" to be "uncomfortably" vague and to allow too much latitude to meaningfulness. He therefore tried to strengthen his "weak" version of the verification principle; see the paperback edition (New York: Dover Publications, 1946), pp. 11–13. Cf. Ferré, *Language*, pp. 12–13, 32–33; Alasdair MacIntyre, "The Logical Status of Religious Belief," in *Metaphysical Beliefs* (London: SCM Press, 1957), p. 171.

[93] Cf. Antony Flew and Alasdair MacIntyre (eds.), *New Essays in Philosophical Theology* (London: SCM Press, paperback ed., 1963), p. vii.

[94] Flew, *New Essays*, pp. 98, 106.

[95] Cf. MacIntyre, "Religious Belief," p. 171; Ferré, *Language*, pp. 32–33.

[96] Flew, *New Essays*, pp. 97–99, 106.

[97] Paul Van Buren, *The Secular Meaning of the Gospel* (New York: Macmillan, 1963), pp. 68, 99–100, 102.

is in principle apprehensible by the senses.[98] One suspects that it is this presupposition which still leads some philosophers and theologians to reject the meaningfulness of statements about God despite the fact that the verification principle is no longer the reigning king in linguistic philosophy.

Verificational analysis gave way to functional analysis, which, if it is not willing to say that theological statements are true, is at least willing to say that they may be meaningful.[99] For functional analysis meaning depends on the *use* of language, and it is recognized that there is a variety of legitimate functions and not just the one[100] of communicating empirical fact.[101] Language will be expected to behave according to the logic of the particular game or frame of reference in which it is operating and not according to the rules of some other game. At the same time there is a certain overlapping of the various games and within each one, a number of legitimate functions.[102] For example, within the theological language game, language may function emotively, performatively, and cognitively. Functional analysis wants to show whether language within any given frame of reference is operating with logical success so that the approach is normative as well as descriptive.[103] Language should behave in a way that is appropriate to its subject matter.

If the verification principle is consciously or tacitly affirmed

[98] Cf. Ferré, *Language*, pp. 43–45, 53–54; William Hordern, *Speaking of God* (New York: Macmillan, 1964), pp. 31–32, 70.

[99] Michael Foster, "Contemporary British Philosophy and Christian Belief," *The Christian Scholar*, 43 (1960), 191. Actually philosophy as philosophy could not affirm that Christian theological statements are true.

[100] Verificational analysis also allowed, of course, the necessity of tautologies or definitions.

[101] Cf. Ferré, *Language*, pp. 55–56, 59; Ferré, in Ferré and Kent Bendall, *Exploring the Logic of Faith* (New York: Association Press, Seminary Paperbacks, 1962), p. 45; MacIntyre, "Religious Belief," pp. 171–172; Hordern, *Speaking*, pp. 40, 42.

[102] Ferré, *Logic*, p. 45; Hordern, *Speaking*, p. 45.

[103] MacIntyre, "Religious Belief," p. 174.

a person may make one of two responses to the Christian faith: (a) He may say that theological statements intend to be assertions about how things are in the universe, but since they cannot be verified one can only reject Christianity.[104] (b) He may say that while theological statements are not assertions about God and how things are, they may function to express the basic presuppositions or perspective or "blik" through which one understands oneself in the world.[105]

Ronald Hepburn draws the category of parable into his "blik" view of religion. The parables of Jesus could presumably serve as parables in his sense, but he would also include the Old Testament and New Testament as a whole as well as plays, novels, and poems. The Bible understood as a parable is not concerned about facts, for a parable can do its work equally well—or better—if it is fictitious.[106] Hepburn assigns to parable the important work of differentiating religion from morality. Religious language as distinguished from moral language provides a tightly cohering parable or myth which vividly expresses a way of life, inspires the believer to implement it, claims the

[104] Flew, *New Essays*, pp. 97, 106, 107–108; Bendall, *Exploring the Logic of Faith*, pp. 11, 16–18, 24–25, 107–109. Bendall disavows positivistic or empiricist criteria but still believes that the evidence for Christianity is not sufficiently public to satisfy "critical intelligence."

[105] R. M. Hare, in *New Essays in Philosophical Theology*, pp. 99–101; Van Buren, *Secular*, pp. 97, 100, 140–142, 169. Van Buren has some helpful insights into the New Testament "blik," and he wants statements which connect the personal pronoun "I" to such words as "free" and "love" to be considered meaningful within the secular gospel (*Secular*, p. 171). Yet he confuses functional analysis with verificational analysis (*ibid.*, pp. 16, 104–105, 131). And it is doubtful whether statements about personal experience (*ibid.*, pp. 131, 147–148), any more than statements about God (*ibid.*, pp. 65, 83), can stand up under his application of the verification principle, that is, testing by sense experience (*ibid.*, p. 65). It cannot be demonstrated by sense experience whether a man really loves or is really free; cf. Dilthey, *Pattern*, p. 164; Ian T. Ramsey, *Religious Language* (New York: Macmillan Paperbacks, 1963), pp. 148–149.

[106] Ronald Hepburn, *Christianity and Paradox* (London: Watts, 1958), pp. 192–193.

believer's total life, and provides his total vision.[107] Here Hepburn comes close to recognizing the aesthetic function of parable, but when he also speaks of the parable as illustrating and exhorting,[108] he tends to detach the meaning from that particular formal structure. This is to vitiate the power of the parable's aesthetic function and to divest the importance which he assigned to it of some of its point.

I believe that the "blik" view is not really an analysis of how users of theological language have usually understood their statements about God. Theological statements do contain a "blik," but the users of Christian language have ordinarily intended to make assertions about God, about how things are in the universe. Theological language properly understood has a cognitive function as well as other functions; it is believing *that* as well as believing *in*.[109] Ott, however, maintains that Christian faith is faith in and not faith that: preaching does not give information. Faith itself, for Ott, includes understanding, and this understanding attains greater clarity in theology, but Ott plays down the cognitive element in both faith and theology in favor of the existential. He conceives of theology on the model of Heidegger's *primal thinking*. For Heidegger primal thinking is that which is called forth from man as a response to being as the latter speaks through beings, unveiling that they are. It is to be distinguished from the objectifying thinking of science and metaphysics, which is self-initiated and

---

[107] *Ibid.*, p. 195.

[108] *Ibid.*, p. 192. It is a little surprising that he does this in view of his perceptive insights into the aesthetic and its function; see his "Poetry and Religious Belief," in *Metaphysical Beliefs*, pp. 139–140.

[109] Cf. I. M. Crombie, "The Possibility of Theological Statements," in *Faith and Logic*, ed. B. Mitchell (London: Allen and Unwin, 1957), pp. 31–32; Ferré, *Language*, p. 160; Ferré, *Logic of Faith*, pp. 66–67; Hordern, *Speaking*, pp. 72–73, 181; Schubert M. Ogden, "Theology and Objectivity," *The Journal of Religion*, 45 (1965), 184–187; Foster, "Christian Belief," pp. 192–193; MacIntyre, "Religious Belief," p. 193.

which observes reality as objects, imposing its (the subject's) categories upon it.[110] Since Ott conceives of theology on the analogy of primal thinking, he denies any strict distinction between faith as existential actuality and theology as thinking.[111] Ott would be unsympathetic with the no-God theology of the thoroughgoing "blik" approach,[112] but his depreciation of the cognitive function of theological language inadvertently shows a certain kinship with that approach and obscures the problem of the relationship between belief in and belief that. It seems to me necessary to affirm the cognitive element in both faith and theology and to account for the difference between the two.

Bultmann and Ebeling also recognize the existential element in theology: it is impossible to speak about God without speaking also about oneself.[113] Theology is the unfolding of faith's own self-understanding, and theological reflection as well as proclamation can offer man an understanding of existence which evokes from him a decision.[114] But at the same time for Bultmann theology paradoxically must speak of faith in objective terms, like any science; and for Ebeling, while theology has its own subject matter, it must reflect scientifically and form concepts, as is done in other fields of thought.[115] The assimilation of theology to faith by Ott would seem to lead to the conclusion either that one must be a believer in order to understand theology or that thinking theological thoughts would make one a believer. Ott rejects these conclusions,[116] but it is difficult to see how they can be avoided unless theology

[110] Cf. Robinson, *Later Heidegger*, pp. 25, 44.
[111] Ott, "Systematic Theology," pp. 90–93, 106–109.
[112] *Ibid.*, p. 90.
[113] Bultmann, "What Sense Is There to Speak of God?" *The Christian Scholar*, 43 (1960), 213, 215; Ebeling, *Word and Faith*, p. 346.
[114] Bultmann, "Case," p. 183; *Theology of the New Testament*, Vol. 2, trans. K. Grobel (London: SCM Press, 1955), pp. 237, 239, 251.
[115] Bultmann, "Case;" p. 193; Ebeling, *Word and Faith*, pp. 248–249, 252.
[116] Ott, "Systematic Theology," p. 92.

as objectifying thought is distinguished from faith.[117] It is not objectifying in the scientific sense of a falsifiable, external perception of a reality which is distinct from ourselves and is the object of sense experience. But theology is objectifying in the same way that the detached analysis of the structure of human existence is objectifying in comparison with existential involvement itself.[118]

Our discussion of the cognitive and objective character of theological language was given in response to the position of verificational analysis that theological language does not make assertions about God. We must now consider further how theological language does make assertions. If we begin, not with the presuppositions of verificational analysis, but with the view that function determines meaning, then we can say that the behavior of theological language points to the kind of subject matter or referent that theological language is talking about.

Theological language begins at the observational level, but this observational language is used with an "odd logic."[119] Adjectives which normally refer to human attitudes or actions —like "good"—are stretched out of their normal usage by qualifiers like "infinite." Assertions are made and then qualified. It is claimed that "God" is an individual, but none of the criteria for individuality are held to apply. Category mistakes are deliberately made.[120] These logical improprieties, however, do not show that theological statements have no referent. They rather give a partial characterization of the referent: God is separate from the spatio-temporal world and yet impinges upon it; as transcendent he is qualitatively different from all other things, and therefore statements about him are not falsi-

---

[117] Cf. Schubert M. Ogden, "The Understanding of Theology in Ott and Bultmann," in *Later Heidegger*, pp. 164–165.
[118] Ogden, "Theology and Objectivity," pp. 178–181.
[119] Ramsey, *Language*, pp. 42, 53.
[120] Ramsey, *Language*, p. 77; Crombie, "Theological Statements," pp. 42, 60; Hordern, *Speaking*, p. 125.

fiable; he is mysterious.[121] The logical behavior of theological language, however, does not give our understanding of God much positive content.

If the odd formal properties of theological language tell us that we are dealing with a mysterious, not wholly knowable, subject or referent, we may follow Crombie in saying that theological statements are given content and related to experience by treating them as parables.[122] We might say that the formal aspects pertain to the subject, and the parabolic aspect pertains to the predicate of theological statements. Crombie would include in his concept of parables such parables proper as The Prodigal Son and such enacted parables as Hosea's seeking out his adulterous wife.[123] His real point, however, is that the comparative or analogical aspect of the parable is the proper category for understanding all theological statements. One does not suppose that there is a literal correspondence between a parable and its referent, but one does suppose that if one accepts the parable as a faithful[124] parable, one will not be misled about the nature of the referent. Thus, for example, we do not know literally what love is in the being of God, but we trust that a parable like The Prodigal Son puts us sufficiently in touch with God to enter into relations with him which bring about our ultimate well-being.[125]

It is important for Crombie's position that the words in our parables about God be taken in their ordinary human sense. The word "love" in "God loves us" is not to be thought of as changed from its ordinary human sense in the way that "hot"

---

[121] Cf. Ramsey, *Language*, p. 84; Crombie, "Theological Statements," pp. 33–34, 38, 49; Ogden, "Theology and Objectivity," pp. 178–179; Hordern, *Speaking*, pp. 119, 124, 125.

[122] Crombie, "Theological Statements," p. 71.

[123] Crombie, in *New Essays in Philosophical Theology*, pp. 119–120.

[124] Cf. Sewell (*Orphic*, p. 21) on the need to have faith in language; also Wheelwright, *Metaphor*, p. 31.

[125] Crombie, "Theological Statements," pp. 70–71; in *New Essays*, p. 124.

in "hot temper" is changed from the ordinary meaning that it has in "hot stove." "Hot" can be thus modified without losing meaning because we already know what temper is apart from that phrase. But we do not already know what God is apart from our parables; therefore, if the predicate words—like "love" —do not have their ordinary meaning, they have very little meaning. But again it must be said that this does not mean that God's love is literally like human love. Rather we believe that parables whose words are taken in their ordinary, human sense put us in touch with a God who is not completely knowable.[126]

Faith, then, has an important place in Crombie's view. We trust the parables because we trust their source—Christ.[127] I think that we would also want and have to say that we trust Christ because his words encounter us as a language event.

The parables of Jesus in their own special way exemplify the features of theological language which we have been discussing. Because of their aesthetic nature they are in certain ways more effective than propositional statements could be, and because of their realistic and dramatic subject matter they give a particular content to our understanding of our relationship with God and tie it to human experience. In the parables the predicate aspect of theological statements is elaborated in terms of dramatic encounters of a particular kind. At the same time

[126] Crombie, in *New Essays*, pp. 120–124; "Theological Statements," p. 72. Ebeling similarly maintains that when the Bible speaks of God's word it means normal, human words as far as their word character is concerned. The difference between the divine word and human words is the difference between a word that is life-giving and a word that is destructive ("Word of God," p. 102). When Ramsey (*Language*, pp. 93–94) denies that theological language works like ordinary language he is not necessarily disagreeing with Crombie, for Ramsey is talking about the odd formal properties which point to the nature of the referent of theological language and not about the parabolic predicates.
[127] Crombie, in *New Essays*, pp. 122–123. Laeuchli (*Language*, p. 247) also warns that within the Christian perspective faith puts a limit on the analysis of language.

there is often in the parables an element of surprise or shock, of the extraordinary, which cuts across the prevailing realism and suggests another dimension of reality which impinges upon the strictly human one. This is analogous to the odd logic of propositional theological statements which points to the mysterious unknowability of their referent.

It has been argued in this section that theological language cannot be verified by sensory experience but that theological statements are still cognitive statements of a certain order of objectivity. They make assertions about God and how things are in the universe. We may go on to say, following Ogden and Ferré, that as objective statements they are of the same class as metaphysical statements and are subject to the kind of verification appropriate to metaphysical statements.[128] A metaphysical system—in the sense meant here—is a structure of concepts which attempts to provide a coherent picture of the whole of reality. A Christian metaphysic would include the Bible as a basic model, image, or configuration which is to a large extent non-propositional. It would also include a systematic interpretation of the Bible in relation to modern thought plus the understanding of God derived from the odd behavior of theological language. A metaphysical system is not to be judged on the basis of its literal correspondence with all of reality but on the basis of whether it provides a perspective from which all facts and experiences can be meaningfully seen.[129] Therefore, an individual belief or concept is to be verified by determining whether it fits into and enhances the whole system; and the system as a whole is to be evaluated or verified on the basis of these criteria: (a) internal consistency; (b) positive coherence of the parts; (c) applicability to experience; (d) illumination of all experience and knowledge without distortion; (e) effec-

---

[128] Ogden, "Theology and Objectivity," p. 190; Ferré, *Language*, p. 160.
[129] Ferré, *Language*, pp. 161–162; *Logic of Faith*, p. 74.

tiveness.[130] It may be supposed that the system which comes the closest to fulfilling these requirements comes the closest to saying what reality is like.

The point has been made sometimes that the poetic quality of biblical images cannot bridge the gap between the coherence and integrating power of biblical language and thought, on the one hand, and the truth of their referent, on the other.[131] There is a sense in which this position is correct, but it is wrong in principle and misses the point both of the odd logic of theological language and of the content of the Christian faith when it is suggested that if the gap can be bridged at all it must be bridged by reasoning.[132] This view ignores the necessity of faith. Some kinds of language are more adequate than others, but the only way to bridge the gap between the most adequate theological language and the certainty of God is by faith. And yet if faith *is* that freedom for the word which the word itself gives when it becomes an event, then it is also true to say that the language event gives certainty of God. The parables as aesthetic objects are particularly apt vehicles for the language event, but the point to remember is that from the Christian standpoint man cannot determine that the preached word or theological thought will become an event.

This insistence on the need for faith does not mean that one must have Christian faith in order to understand the Christian perspective, but one must have faith if the Christian perspective is to become the self-understanding which structures one's existence, or, rather, letting one's existence be so structured is faith. This does not relieve the Christian theologian-metaphysician from making his system as adequate as possible, but

---

[130] Ferré, *Language*, pp. 162–163; *Logic of Faith*, p. 74; cf. MacIntyre, "Religious Belief," p. 202.
[131] Cf. Hepburn, "Poetry," p. 165.
[132] *Ibid.*, pp. 165–166.

there are competing metaphysical systems, so that a point is reached where one must make a commitment which never escapes the character of a risk or wager. This does not mean that Christian faith is flying in the face of the evidence. It rather means that a response is made to a particular body of evidence that "convicts" us by "proving itself."[133] The response remains a risk because one cannot be unaware that there are other convictors around.

Theological knowledge is not different from other kinds of knowledge in this regard. The acceptance of any basic perspective always involves a decision about what is evidence.[134] As Polanyi has forcefully argued, any knowledge comes to be held as true through the inarticulate and personal factor which shapes and organizes knowledge.[135] And for Wheelwright[136] taking a statement as true depends on having a conviction that one ought to assent to it.

One of the criteria of an adequate metaphysical system is that it should effectively come to life. To come to life it must be understood, and understanding involves seeing the parts as a comprehensive whole or gestalt or configuration.[137] The parables are especially important in this connection because as aesthetic objects they *are* gestalten. Thus, as a gestalt, a parable presents a large part of the essential pattern of the total perspective in a pre-conceptual but highly concentrated way. This is another way of saying that the parables have a particularly high potential for becoming the language events which put one in the stance of faith or evoke the willingness to take a risk.

In addition the interpretive translation of the parables' understanding of existence contributes to the effort to work out

[133] Hordern, *Speaking*, pp. 98, 113; MacIntyre, "Religious Belief," p. 202.
[134] Hordern, *Speaking*, pp. 70, 101–102.
[135] Michael Polanyi, *The Study of Man* (Chicago: The University of Chicago Press, Phoenix Books, 1963), pp. 25–26, 28.
[136] *Fountain*, pp. 287–289.
[137] Polanyi, *Man*, pp. 28, 44. Recall also Dilthey.

a Christian metaphysic. The demand to give a full existential translation of the parables—in the pregnant sense which contemporary hermeneutic gives to the term "translation"—is grounded in the existential necessity of living a unified existence.[138] The man who responds to the language event of the parables must relate his response and its implications to what and how he thinks about the whole of reality. This chapter began by noticing that hermeneutic is grounded in the biblical understanding of history, and it ends by noting that hermeneutic is grounded in the biblical understanding of existence. There is no contradiction, for the biblical understandings of history and of human existence are two sides of the same thing.

[138] Space does not allow a full presentation of the New Testament's drive for a unified existence, but one example may be mentioned. It is seen in the pervasive and paradoxical union of the indicative and imperative. The man of faith is to become what he is, which presupposes that he should have an integrated existence.

3

The Parables, Aesthetics, and Literary Criticism

In the two preceding chapters it has been assumed that certain of the parables of Jesus are aesthetic in nature, but very little has been done to define the aesthetic or to demonstrate that the parables are in fact aesthetic objects, genuine works of art. It is now necessary to attempt in detail such a definition and such a demonstration.

This effort will involve a battle on two fronts: (a) Over against the main tendencies in New Testament scholarship it must be shown that a parable as an aesthetic object should not be treated as an illustration of an idea or a dressing out of a "point." (b) Over against certain dominant tendencies in literary criticism it must be shown that while the parables have an existential-theological dimension they are, nevertheless, genuine aesthetic objects.

The latter effort would not be such a problem within the perspective of the "old criticism," which holds that literature exists, not in isolation, but within the play of historical and political forces and that it has a philosophical and theological range and temper.[1] It is, however, a problem over against the "new criticism" which has been dominant for the last several decades. This critical approach has emphasized that a literary

[1] Cf. George Steiner, *Tolstoy or Dostoevsky* (New York: Random House, Vintage Books, 1961), pp. 6–7.

work as aesthetic is autonomous—detached from sociological and psychological phenomena and from any independent and articulated system of thought—"an absolutely self-contained and discrete set of mutually inter-related references."[2] How then can the parables have an existential-theological subject matter and still be aesthetic objects? The argument vis-à-vis new criticism will have two prongs. First it will attempt to show that all literature contains *inherently*, even though implicitly and indirectly, a thought dimension—a world view or understanding of existence (sections 1–3). And secondly it will seek to demonstrate that the parables have qualities which make them genuinely aesthetic (sections 4–5).

It is true that quite recently the absolute autonomy of the literary work has been questioned, and by critics who have belonged to the new critical tradition, but they are by no means abandoning the belief that the aesthetic object is in some important sense autonomous, nor should they. We must, therefore, try to reach an understanding of what aesthetic autonomy can properly mean.[3] It may appear that too much attention is given to defining the aesthetic object as such, but all of the points are relevant to our understanding of the parables.

1. Language as Symbol

The nature of language as such will be briefly considered—insofar as it is necessary for distinguishing the aesthetic and

---

[2] Nathan A. Scott, Jr., *The Climate of Faith in Modern Literature* (New York: Seabury Press, 1964), p. xii. Scott questions whether literature is this.

[3] The position of Eliseo Vivas will serve as a kind of touchstone for a definition of the aesthetic, not because his is the only aesthetic theory available but because it is intrinsically valuable and also especially pertinent in connection with the problem of autonomy. While Vivas disclaims being *the* aesthetician of the contextualist—or new—critics, he does assent to a close relationship between his views and the practice of the new critics *(The Artistic Transaction*, p. 172), a relationship pointed out in Murray Krieger, *The New Apologists for Poetry* (Minneapolis: University of Minnesota Press, 1956), p. 129.

propositional uses of language. We may agree that there is a "basic symbolic activity"[4] or "primary imagination"[5] which enables us to grasp the phenomena of the world, to constitute the world as a meaningful whole. According to Eliseo Vivas this basic symbolic activity—with language being our most important symbol—underlies the four modes of experience— aesthetic, cognitive, moral, and religious—which exhaust the human possibilities.[6]

What, more precisely, is the symbolic nature of language and how does it enable us to grasp the world? In Wheelwright's view a symbol is that which means, or conveys meaning, and a word as a symbol means by pointing or making reference to that which is no longer sensuously present. The word stands for something.[7] Vivas, on the other hand, calls language at this level a sign rather than a symbol. It is his position that a symbol means itself or has an immanent, reflexive, non-referential meaning before it can mean something else or be a sign.[8] But in reply to Vivas it must be said that even if language first occurred as a complex of interrelated symbols[9] and not as a means for isolating individual objects, surely the first words had meaning by association with external and internal objects and not as sounds in themselves. Language came into existence as a bridge between the inner world of mind and outer existence, as a pointer to the latter, and arose from the capacity to separate these two.[10] Polanyi has argued that words, maps, and sym-

[4] Vivas, *Transaction*, pp. 9, 14, 16.

[5] Philip Wheelwright, *The Burning Fountain*, pp. 18, 77–78.

[6] Vivas, *Transaction*, pp. 9–10.

[7] Wheelwright, *Fountain*, pp. 18–19, 23–24.

[8] Eliseo Vivas, *D. H. Lawrence: The Failure and Triumph of Art* (Evanston: Northwestern University Press, 1960), pp. 276–277.

[9] As Vivas claims (*Transaction*, pp. 34–35).

[10] Cf. Rollo May, "The Significance of Symbols," in *Symbolism in Religion and Literature*, ed. R. May (New York: George Braziller, 1960), pp. 21–22; Erich Kahler, "The Nature of Symbol," in *Symbolism in Religion and Literature*, pp. 54–57; Elizabeth Sewell, *The Orphic Voice*, pp. 28–29.

bols are never objects of attention in themselves but are instruments of meaning by pointing toward the things which they mean, that is, which they stand for. To shift attention to the word or symbol as an object viewed in itself destroys the meaning. Repeat the word "table" twenty times, and it becomes an empty sound.[11] At the same time the very fact that there *are* words means that the object to which a word points may be considered without our having to visualize or turn our attention to the object. Language fixes or "freezes" meaning as an entity separate from the object or referent so that it does not merely point but also represents and acquires a certain autonomy.[12]

Thus at the most basic level a word as a pointer has a "through-meaning," and as a frozen or autonomous focus of attention it has an "in-meaning." The point to be developed in the next two sections is that as linguistic development and organization become complex, the aesthetic use of language draws more strongly on the "in-meaning" of language while the propositional or non-aesthetic draws more strongly on the "through-meaning."

2. The Organic Unity and Autonomy of the Aesthetic Object

(1) Aesthetic experience is a particular and unique type of experience of a correlative type of object. That is to say, it is the experience of intransitive, non-referential, or rapt *attention* to an object which is capable of evoking that kind of experience. In non-aesthetic modes of experience attention is transitive; that is, it is referred beyond the object of concern to other objects and meanings. In reading a scientific treatise one is referred to the phenomena which it describes and to other treatises about them. In evaluating a moral act one may wonder

[11] Michael Polanyi, *The Study of Man*, p. 30. According to Polanyi, saying that a symbol is its own meaning is a category mistake (*ibid.*, p. 65).
[12] Kahler, "Symbol," pp. 54–57; Vivas, *Transaction*, p. 36.

about the motives which prompted it. And in Christian worship one is referred beyond the sacramental occurrences to the historical and ontological realities which they represent, though that is not all that one would want to say about the Christian sacraments. In aesthetic experience, however, the attention is totally engaged by and riveted on the object itself—at least as an ideal. During the successful aesthetic experience the play, painting, music, or whatever is the beholder's whole world, and his attention is not referred beyond it.[13]

The aesthetic object must be such that it can grasp our attention non-referentially despite the fact that it may contain thoughts, values, or images which are unacceptable or uninteresting to us outside of aesthetic experience.[14] A literary work is able to grasp attention intransitively because it does not refer to actions and thoughts which exist in the real world nor does it even imitate the phenomenal world. It is not just a slice of life but rather presents actions and thoughts which are imaginative, fictitious, hypothetical, and potential.[15] This imaginative and hypothetical element obtains even if a work of fiction makes some use of historical events, for those events will be taken up into a new context or configuration which will give them a different meaning than they had in history. Thus the most far-reaching differentia of a work of literary art is its form or shape or organization or pattern of connections. It is not organized so as to elicit a train of thought that moves beyond itself. Rather when language is used aesthetically, the form—that to which all of the elements relate—is centripetally organized so that all of the parts tightly cohere with each other.

---

[13] Vivas, *Transaction*, pp. 12, 17, 19–32, 38; *Creation and Discovery* (New York: Noonday Press, 1955), pp. xi, 93–97; Kahler, "Symbol," pp. 60–61; Wheelwright, *Fountain*, pp. 60–61.

[14] Vivas, *Transaction*, p. 61.

[15] Cf. Northrop Frye, *Anatomy of Criticism*, pp. 63–64, 80, 93; René Wellek and Austin Warren, *Theory of Literature* (New York: Harcourt, Brace, and World, Harvest Books, 1956), pp. 14–15.

Words, meanings, and actions do not point out to the world beyond but are interlocked with each other. Thus the form serves as a frame which gives to the literary work a certain distance from the world. This organically and inwardly unified form keeps the beholder's attention moving from one part of the work to another and not to the outside.[16]

The organic unity of the literary work means that while form and content may be distinguished they are not separable in the work itself. In a story the events are a part of the content, and the way they are arranged into a plot is a part of the form. The form is the organization of the matter. Change the arrangement, and you have something else.[17] Form and content are welded together—content is informed—by new combinations and juxtapositions of words which put a strain on normal dictionary meanings and create tension. Such a tension-generating combination is what Wheelwright means by "metaphor" and Brooks by "paradox."[18] The important point is that new meanings emerge and the literary work is the unique and organic thing which it is just through such extraordinary combinations. Break up the combination, and the new meaning is dissolved. Therefore, metaphor and paradox are not simply a pretty and gilded way of saying something that could be said in other words but the necessary and inevitable tools of the literary artist.[19]

[16] Cf. Vivas, *Transaction*, pp. 49–51, 57, 63, 157–159; Wellek and Warren, *Literature*, pp. 13, 175, 231; Frye, *Anatomy*, pp. 77–78, 82–83.

[17] Wellek and Warren, *Literature*, pp. 128–129, 231.

[18] Wheelwright, *Fountain*, pp. 101, 105; *Metaphor and Reality*, pp. 70–90; Cleanth Brooks, "The Language of Paradox," *American Literary Criticism*, ed. C. I. Glicksberg (New York: Hendricks House, 1951), pp. 520–528; cf. also Wellek and Warren, *Literature*, pp. 169–170, 182.

[19] Cf. Brooks, "Paradox," p. 528; "Metaphor and the Function of Criticism," in *Spiritual Problems in Contemporary Literature*, ed. S. R. Hopper (New York: Harper Torchbooks, 1957), pp. 133–134. The new critical position would not accept the opinion of R. Hepburn ("Poetry and Religious Belief," p. 152) that the paradoxes in literature can be more or less successfully reduced to a paraphrase.

We could say in view of the organic unity of the literary work that its meaning resides in the form-and-content as a whole. This closely parallels the position of Polanyi that understanding occurs when we are focally aware of a total gestalt or configuration and subsidiarily aware of its particular parts.[20] From the aesthetic standpoint, to isolate one element in a literary work for special consideration breaks the unity of the work and obscures the meaning of that element by removing it from the context which provides its meaning. This is underlined by Polanyi's view that comprehension may be destroyed by shifting focal attention from the gestalt to one of the subsidiary particulars.[21]

A point made by Elizabeth Sewell indicates why language used aesthetically grasps the attention in a way that propositional discourse does not. She has pointed out that the term "form" includes both the ideas of abstraction and of bodily shape and has suggested that the formal activity of the mind-body may have its roots in the physical. Thus form—especially when content is incarnated in it—addresses itself both to body and mind.[22] We have here a kind of correlation of the unity of mind and body with the unity of content and shape in form. In language used aesthetically the content depends on the shape or pattern of connections in a way that it does not in propositional or analytical discourse. Therefore, man in his psychosomatic wholeness is addressed more completely in literary works than in non-aesthetic discourse: because in the former the palpable, shaping factor of the body itself is more fully present. The union of form and content speaks to the union of body and mind. Thus not only is thought called forth, but those forces of the self which are ulterior to the conscious are also engaged.

20 Polanyi, *Man*, pp. 29–30, 32, 44; cf. also May, "Symbols," p. 34.
21 Polanyi, *Man*, pp. 28, 32.
22 Sewell, *Orphic*, pp. 34–39.

(2) Because the literary work is fictitious and is an inwardly organized structure capable of attracting non-referential attention, it is also autonomous. The latter point was implied in the preceding discussion of the literary work's organic unity, for organicism and autonomy are two sides of the same reality. Several aspects of autonomy need, however, to be spelled out.

As autonomous, the literary work is independent of its author. It has links with his life, but these are of no critical importance, because they are fused into the new configuration which the work is. Works of literary art reveal something that cannot be traced to the author's biography or environment.[23] His intention "is neither available nor desirable as a standard for judging the success" of the work. The only important consideration is the internal meaning of the work itself.[24] If the mother of a work of art is nature, the author is not the father but is rather the womb or midwife while the father is the forms and conventions which the author inherits from the literary tradition.[25] This point affirms the autonomy of the work in relation to the author but not in relation to the literary tradition; however, the dependence of a work on the latter has also been denied.[26]

If the interpreter should not commit the "intentional fallacy" of seeking a work's meaning in the author's intention, neither should he commit the "affective fallacy" of confusing the work with its psychological effects in the reader. The mis-

[23] Vivas, *Creation*, p. x; Wellek and Warren, *Literature*, pp. 66–68.
[24] William K. Wimsatt and Monroe C. Beardsley, *The Verbal Icon* (Lexington: University of Kentucky Press, 1954), pp. 3–4, 10. There is an analogy between this position and Barth's view of verbal inspiration as James D. Smart interprets it (*The Interpretation of Scripture*, pp. 195–196). Revelation is in the text itself and not in a history or biography that can be constructed from it.
[25] Frye, *Anatomy*, p. 98; cf. also Wellek and Warren, *Literature*, pp. 66–67.
[26] Vivas, *Transaction*, pp. 256–257; cf. also Murray Krieger, *A Window to Criticism* (Princeton: Princeton University Press, 1964), pp. 42–48, 52–53.

guided affective criticism makes such statements as "To read this book is like living through an experience." It is not to be denied that a work may have a heightening effect on the reader's consciousness, but pointing that out is no part of the objective critical interpretation of the work.[27]

It has also been held that literary art is autonomous in relation to thought and society. Philosophical and theological ideas, moral values, and social phenomena as the sociologist sees them are not intrinsic elements in an aesthetic object. Nor is it even proper to use the terms "truth" and "knowledge" with reference to the aesthetic. Art is intrinsically autotelic, not a means but an end.[28] If the artistic work is such a self-contained world of new word combinations, then the belief that it could be successfully rendered into other words or paraphrased can only be labeled heresy. The conceptualizing, or turning into other terms, of a work of art is always something other than the work itself, for what the latter says can be said in no other way.[29]

Murray Krieger has claimed that the new critics for the most part have not with sufficient consistency maintained the organic and autonomous nature of literary art. It appears to be Krieger's position (in an earlier book) that the literary work cannot be partly closed—with all of its parts interlocked centripetally into each other—and also partly open—referring to the world and to thought. The contextual system of the work should be kept closed so that the reader will have to find his way into it "by its *seeming* use of ordinary reference" (my

[27] Wimsatt and Beardsley, *Icon*, pp. 21, 30, 32.

[28] Vivas, *Transaction*, pp. 41, 63–68, 209–210, 235–236; Wellek and Warren, *Literature*, pp. 91–92, 98–99, 104, 112–113, 175, 229; Frye, *Anatomy*, p. 75.

[29] Cf. Vivas, *Transaction*, p. 68; *Lawrence*, p. 281; Cleanth Brooks, "Implications of an Organic Theory of Poetry," in *Literature and Belief*, ed. M. H. Abrams (New York: Columbia University Press, 1958), pp. 62–63; R. P. Blackmur, "A Critic's Job of Work," in *American Literary Criticism*, pp. 388–389.

italics). The reader is kept within the work "bouncing from opposition to opposition." In a good literary work no conceptualizing, all-reconciling synthesis is possible because every self or claim is met by a counterclaim.[30]

The autonomous theory of literary art will have to be given some criticism in the next section. But before leaving this one, it might be well to state a summary conclusion about the aesthetic object which can stand in the main despite the coming criticisms: The peculiar function of language used aesthetically is that through its centripetal interlocking of content into form it grasps the attention of the beholder as a total psychosomatic unity—including conscious and unconscious aspects—in an intransitive or non-referential way.

3. The Aesthetic Object and the World of Life and Thought

I think that it is beyond question that a work of literary art, as contrasted with propositional discourse, has primarily an "in-meaning" (developed in the previous section) rather than a "through-meaning" or pointing meaning. But does the organic unity of the work give to it the straightforward and unequivocal autonomy which has sometimes been claimed? The various elements are given a new context and frame of reference, to be sure, but in themselves they still relate in some way to what is already known. Otherwise there would be no communication. Nor have the most ardent new or contextualist critics—even Krieger—developed their position consistently. Sometimes those who hold to the autonomy of art also state that the formalistic criticism which emphasizes autonomy is not the whole story and that a literary work somehow contains a *Weltanschauung* which must confront the truth and knowledge of experience.[31]

---

[30] Murray Krieger, *The Tragic Vision* (New York: Holt, Rinehart, and Winston, 1960), pp. 233–242.
[31] Cf. Frye, *Anatomy*, p. 115; Wellek and Warren, *Literature*, pp. 7, 21–23, 82, 104, 140, 203–204, 236–237.

But *how* the literary work can have meaning both *in* and *through* itself is not always made as clear as might be desired. Before attempting such a clarification, however, we must consider further the ambiguity and instability which one often finds in the autonomy position.

For example, the theological and philosophical interpretation of Kafka is decried by a critic who states that a literary analysis shows the Kafkan mode of writing to be a continuous oscillation of hope and despair.[32] Does not the apparent impossibility of avoiding theological-philosophical terms in a literary analysis suggest that the theological and literary aspects of a work cannot be easily separated? Vivas affirms that art and life penetrate each other and cannot be separated since life is the matter of art and art constitutes the world for us. But one wonders whether the dominant tendency of his position allows the above affirmation. He holds, on the one hand, that the tragic quality of certain works is "the stuff of life," including the understanding that man is flawed and resides in a flawed cosmos, while, on the other hand, he maintains that moral and existential truths are only derived and abstracted from literature. Or again, he states that the success of the aesthetic experience depends in part "on the intrinsic worth of the meanings and values embodied," on the substance of the work, and that the meanings must be satisfactory in order for the work to be significant. But he ends by claiming that artistic significance depends, not on moral, religious, or truth values, which could be conceptualized, but on the work's capacity to inform our affective processes or to absorb us. It is the latter view which is more consistent with the overall logic of his position that art is autotelic;[33] yet he does not avoid altogether attributing to

[32] H. S. Reiss, "Recent Kafka Criticism (1944–1955)—A Survey," in *Kafka*, ed. R. Gray (Englewood Cliffs: Prentice-Hall, 1962), pp. 163–165, 172.

[33] Vivas, *Transaction*, pp. 7, 57–58, 67–68, 76–77, 117, 131, 135, 174–175; *Creation*, pp. x, xi, 123–124.

literary works a conceptual meaning. Krieger holds that a literary work is closed in the sense that it cannot be reduced to a consistent, propositional paraphrase which points to an independent system of thought, and at times he appears to deny that it is in any way referentially open at all. Yet it is also his position that the irreconcilable oppositions within the literary work are reflections of and reflectors onto the "Manichean" antitheses of existence itself.[34] Perhaps he means that the conflict of meanings and values in the work points to the similar conflict in life in a formal, and not material, way; but it is still a pointing.

In view of such ambiguity it is not surprising that some of the most recent criticism has rejected the claim of absolute autonomy and recognized the relevance of biographical, historical, and philosophical factors for interpretation.[35] G. Ingli James, moreover, has convincingly put his finger on a major source of the instability. In theory a critic may hold the absolute autonomy view—going back to the French symbolists—which says that art should not try to communicate with other men at all but is a dialogue of a mind with itself. This view presupposes an existential understanding which holds that the only two alternatives for man are isolated individualism or submergence in the collective. The same critic, however, in practice may work with a view of autonomy which says that while a work of art cannot be reduced to a paraphrase, nevertheless, since art appeals to the whole man, including his intellect, it is not impossible nor illegitimate to extract a conceptual meaning, which can be related to the world of thought in general. This view presupposes an understanding of existence which says that

---

[34] Krieger, *Tragic*, pp. 236–237, 242–244.

[35] Cf. *Learners and Discerners: A Newer Criticism*, ed. Robert Scholes (Charlottesville: The University Press of Virginia, 1964), pp. v, vi, 18, 23, 25, 64; Scott, *Climate*, pp. xiii, xiv.

a person most fully realizes his individuality through participation in inter-human relationships.[36]

If we cannot escape the presence of a conceptual meaning or "through-meaning" in a literary work, how is its presence to be accounted for in view of the centripetal organization of language used aesthetically? We noted earlier that language at the most basic level has an inalienable "sign," "pointing," or "through" aspect; and this persists even when words are put together aesthetically. Thus the words of a novel, say, point out to objects—whether things or concepts—that have a more general meaning than the new, particular meaning given by the form of the novel; and the two meanings are not completely discontinuous.[37] Furthermore, it may be questioned whether the interlocking organization of a literary work *could* keep our attention moving among elements which were completely unfamiliar to us from the phenomenal world.[38]

In addition it must be said that the aesthetically organized form or pattern of connections itself contains implicitly a perspective on life or understanding of existence.[39] Indeed, as we have noticed, understanding as such consists precisely in grasping a comprehensive whole or gestalt while being subsidiarily aware of the parts as clues.[40] Thus aesthetic experience participates in the very nature of understanding. The reader

[36] G. Ingli James, "The Autonomy of the Work of Art: Modern Criticism and the Christian Tradition," in *The New Orpheus*, ed. Nathan A. Scott, Jr. (New York: Sheed and Ward, 1964), pp. 194–195, 200–206. Erich Auerbach (*Mimesis*, pp. 444–445) attributes the absoluteness and isolation of pure aesthetics to the nineteenth-century artist's aversion to his bourgeois audience.

[37] Cf. Kahler, "Symbol," p. 67; Wheelwright, *Metaphor*, pp. 28–29, 49–50; Blackmur, "Critic's," p. 402; Hepburn, "Poetry," p. 97.

[38] Cf. Frederick Ferré, *Language, Logic, and God*, pp. 128, 147.

[39] Cf. Wheelwright, *Fountain*, pp. 296–302, 331; *Metaphor*, p. 16; N. Scott, *Modern Literature and the Religious Frontier* (New York: Harper, 1958), pp. 32–36; Helen Gardner, *The Limits of Literary Criticism* (London: Oxford University Press, 1956), pp. 18–19.

[40] Cf. Polanyi, *Man*, pp. 26–29.

of a novel will inevitably, at some level of consciousness, relate the implicit understanding of existence in the story to the understanding which he already has. In aesthetic experience, then, our attention moves both *within* the pattern of connections of the aesthetic object itself and also to the *outside*[41] as we notice the connection between a mountain in a painting and a mountain that we have seen or the relationship between the implied existential understanding in the form of a novel and our own view of things.

The literary work as an autonomous focus of attention means (has meaning) in itself and, as a pointer, means through itself. The inseparability of the two ways of meaning corresponds to the inseparable unity of body and mind in man. The human organism is a body that thinks, and in all thinking the mind unites with a figure—language—of its own devising.[42] The form-aspect of language corresponds to the shaping tendency of the body and the substance-aspect to the centrifugal tendency of discursive reason. But the two aspects cannot be separated either in language or in man;[43] yet they are not present in the same proportion in analytical and aesthetic linguistic experience. Vivas also speaks of art as meaning both in and through itself, but his theory does not adequately account for the "through-meaning" and thus involves him in inconsistency. His fundamental error, I believe, is attributing to man's basic symbolic activity only an "in" (or non-referential) meaning and then giving to the aesthetic a privileged relationship to the basic symbolic activity.

The attempt to account for the presence of both an "in-meaning" and a "through-meaning" by returning to the con-

[41] Cf. Frye, *Anatomy*, pp. 73–74; Wheelwright, *Fountain*, pp. 47–50, 147–154; *Metaphor*, pp. 167–168.

[42] Sewell, *Orphic*, pp. 19–20.

[43] Cf. Amos N. Wilder, *Early Christian Rhetoric*, p. 33; James, "Autonomy," pp. 204–205.

cept of allegory[44] does not seem helpful. To see a literary work as an allegory vitiates its proper autonomy. On the other hand, when Honig asserts in effect that a work is both allegorical and autonomous[45] he contradicts his own definition of an allegory as a twice-told tale which draws its pattern from an old story.[46] We are on better grounds with Michael Novak[47] who tells us that fiction presents, not a philosophy, but the living through of an experience within a certain horizon, with the horizon being pre-philosophical. Krieger has offered a most helpful and fruitful way of relating the literary work to the world of life and thought while protecting its legitimate autonomy. If the work operates properly, it is related to the world sequentially as window, mirror, and window. First it is a set of windows through which we see the familiar world referentially. Then the windows become mirrors reflecting inwardly on each other. In this set of reflecting mirrors the familiar and the hitherto unperceived are organized in a new pattern of connections so that in this pattern there is an implicit or pre-conceptual existential understanding. Finally the mirrors become windows again giving us a new vision of the world. Thus the work, being at once word and world, leads both somewhere else and terminally to itself. But even as window the second time the work still offers a pre-conceptual understanding, and the latter is conceptualized only in criticism.[48]

This represents a move beyond, or at least a clarification of, Krieger's earlier position. Formerly he spoke of a work's making seeming reference to the world,[49] but now he speaks of actual reference, though this is not the most important thing.

[44] As in Edwin Honig, *Dark Conceit*.
[45] *Ibid.*, pp. 93, 96, 113, 125, 181–182.
[46] *Ibid.*, p. 12.
[47] "Philosophy and Fiction," p. 101.
[48] Krieger, *Window*, pp. 30–31, 33–36, 59–65; cf. Scott, *Climate*, pp. 10–11.
[49] Krieger, *Tragic*, p. 237.

Earlier he denied that a work can be both open and closed[50] while now he speaks of the category of "miracle" as necessary to account for the fact that it is both open and closed, both window and mirror.[51]

Heinrich Ott, speaking from the theologian's side, sounds very much like Krieger. A poem speaks out of one reality and into another which is the same. It speaks out of the old world, but by substituting a new pattern it establishes a new world, which is the old world seen in a new way. There is a transition or crossing over in which the speech-world of the word and the so-called "outer world" merge into a single level of reality. It is not that the poem is an indication of something outside itself, but rather when it is spoken and heard the reality which it contains occurs or happens.[52] We could say, then, that Krieger's miracle is a language event. The shape of the world as represented in a literary work may confront the reader with a decision about what the structure of his world is to be and carry him across the crisis of conflict into the new world of the work.

With reference to the effort of the new criticism to avoid the affective fallacy, it should be noted that the rejection of affective criticism makes the notion of the language event adventitious to the meaning of a literary work. But if various literary forms and various examples of a particular form differ in their capacity to become events, then it would seem that the question of wherein such capacity lies cannot be merely extrinsic in evaluating the total meaning of a work. Especially is this true in view of the essentially linguistic nature of human existence. If existence itself is to a considerable degree structured by our understanding of it, which occurs through lan-

---

[50] *Ibid.*, p. 236.
[51] Krieger, *Window*, p. 39.
[52] Heinrich Ott, "The Problem of Non-objectifying Thinking and Speaking in Theology," pp. 5–8.

guage, then it is an important matter whether a particular linguistic object has the capacity to become an event—to give us a new structure of understanding—and hence to change our existence.

In this chapter it has been argued that a work of literary art means both in and through itself but that the inner, non-referential meaning is dominant. That it has both of these aspects but that the one is dominant is greatly illuminated by Polanyi's distinction between focal and subsidiary awareness or attention. In considering the relationship of the whole of a literary work to its parts Polanyi's position was applied above so as to affirm that one should be focally aware of the total structure and subsidiarily aware of the individual parts. Turning now to the question of the relationship of a work of art to the world of life and thought, it must be said that Polanyi's view of symbols in one place appears to be that one should always be subsidiarily aware of the symbol and focally aware of that to which it points.[53] However, in another place[54] he may at least imply that in aesthetic experience one is focally aware of the aesthetic object, the symbol. In any case it is necessary to assert the latter point in order to do justice to the difference between aesthetic and non-aesthetic linguistic experience. In non-aesthetic reading we *are* subsidiarily aware of the language and focally aware of what is being pointed to. But in aesthetic linguistic experience we are focally aware of the linguistic structure and subsidiarily aware of any pointing outward to the world. Thus Polanyi's distinction enables us to differentiate an aesthetic linguistic object from a non-aesthetic one.

The position taken in the preceding paragraph means that it is an overstatement to claim that in aesthetic experience

[53] Polanyi, *Man*, pp. 30, 44.
[54] Michael Polanyi, *Personal Knowledge* (rev. ed.; New York and Evanston: Harper Torchbooks, 1964), pp. 193–194.

the attention is intransitively or non-referentially engaged, for actually the attention is divided. As we noticed, however, it is not divided the same way in aesthetic experience that it is in non-aesthetic. In a truly aesthetic piece of narrative fiction the centripetal interlocking of the parts will keep the attention focally on the work itself. But the reader will be subsidiarily aware—aware at lower levels of consciousness[55]— of various kinds of pointing outward to the world outside the narrative. This understanding of the divided attention shows why the inevitable presence of elements that point outward, that is, of allegorical elements, need not turn a work into an allegory. When content is skillfully informed, focal attention may be kept on the work itself, although subsidiary attention is given to certain elements that point outward. If, however, an individual part or the philosophical orientation becomes so obvious as to draw attention focally to itself, then the organic unity of the work is shattered, and we have something approaching an allegory.

In fiction the focus of attention is the total narrative configuration, while the pointing outward to another frame of reference by an individual element is subsidiary and addresses a much lower level of consciousness. In between these two is the work's understanding of existence. In relation to the pattern of events this understanding is subsidiary and implicit, and being implicit it is pre-conceptual. But it is more nearly focal than an individual element because it is implicit in the work as a whole. And being implicit *in* the pattern composed of the order of events and the characters' awareness, the existential understanding is an inherent part of the work. Theological and philosophical views of how and why things happen as they do, if they are fused into the work's internal coherence, are not extra-aesthetic. Therefore, being made aware of an understand-

[55] Cf. Polanyi, *Man*, pp. 44–45.

ing of existence is an inherent, though subsidiary, part of aesthetic experience as such.

With reference to the parables of Jesus we would then say that focal attention should be on the whole narrative pattern and attention somewhat less focal on the implied understanding of existence. The reference of individual points to Jesus' ministry should receive only subsidiary attention. Or to be more accurate, when Jesus told the parables, the story itself probably did engage the hearers' attention focally while the pointing of certain elements in the story to aspects of Jesus' ministry evoked only subsidiary attention. When the meaning of the parable as a whole is grasped, however, it is a window through which we may see the world anew.

4. The Parables as Aesthetic Objects

This section will assume that what was said about the nature of the aesthetic object in the two previous sections applies in essentials to the parables (though a demonstration of the parables' aesthetic nature awaits the next section) and will seek to show how the disregarding of their aesthetic nature nullifies much of their proper function. One cannot imagine a more pointed denial of the parables' aesthetic quality than that found in Oesterley. According to him the form is of no consequence and everything is concentrated in the purpose for which the parable was told. The form is "merely" a "casket" for "holding the treasure" and is not even to be considered "in view of the real thing within it."[56] This is a glaring denial of the centripetally organized unity of form and content which characterizes an aesthetic object. We may rarely find this position so sharply stated, yet it is tacitly the guiding principle of the one-point approach to the parables. Let us

[56] W. O. E. Oesterley, *The Gospel Parables in the Light of Their Jewish Background*, p. 82.

now look at two recent discussions which offer somewhat more promise but do not consistently follow through.

Linnemann recognizes that a parable is not simply derived from Jesus' historical situation, that despite close correspondences with the latter the story is self-sustaining and thus has a certain autonomy.[57] Yet she insists that the real meaning of a parable is the one point of comparison that links it with Jesus' historical situation, which is the clue to its meaning.[58] Linnemann goes on to argue that the economy of description and narrative development in a parable—for example, we do not learn whether the elder son was moved to share his father's joy—has the intention of deflecting attention from the story to the historical situation.[59] Thus she is claiming that the parables are intentionally non-aesthetic.

Against Linnemann it must be said that even if it was Jesus' intention—which is doubtful—to deflect attention immediately from the parable to the situation, in many cases it would not have happened. A number of the parables are sufficiently well developed aesthetically—that is, have their content sufficiently well informed—to attract the focal attention of the hearer non-referentially. At the same time, Auerbach[60] suggests that economy of description may heighten rather than lessen the power of a story to grasp the attention.

The one-point approach goes hand in hand with the severely historical method. It sees the meaning of the parable in one isolated factor which is connected with a situation outside of the parable, thus shattering the parable's aesthetic unity. The one-point, historical methodology fails to see that form exercises a pressure on matter or content, pushing the elements

---

[57] Eta Linnemann, *Die Gleichnisse Jesu*, pp. 32–33, 36–37.
[58] *Ibid.*, pp. 26, 32, 37–38.
[59] *Ibid.*, pp. 21, 28.
[60] *Mimesis*, pp. 7–9.

together, so to speak, and diffusing the meaning throughout the whole. Since this is the case, one cannot simply lift the meaning out as if it were a drop of oil in water, for it is spread throughout the texture of the whole parable.

G. V. Jones recognizes that Jesus' parables are art forms and that as such they are not propositional statements. As works of art they "combine character and idea with pattern," and the pressure of the form gives some autonomy from the historical situation of origin.[61] This good insight is not clearly worked out by Jones, however, and the ambiguity of his position is seen in his classification of the parables. He has three classes: (a) Those parables that have little or no meaning apart from their historical setting. (b) "Those which are capable of only one interpretation, because they illustrate some particular teaching" and "cannot be legitimately applied to anything else," yet were not evoked by any particular situation. (c) Those which arose out of a historical situation but are capable of a wider interpretation or application to circumstances different from those of origin.[62]

Although Jones recognizes the importance of pattern or form in art, he classifies the parables, not according to the degree of formal development nor according to the type of form, but rather according to what he takes to be their content. Moreover, he places fully developed narrative parables in all three of his classes. It is his view that those in group one (including The Workers in the Vineyard, The Ten Maidens, The Unjust Steward, and The Wicked Tenants) have no relevance in themselves for later situations and can be made relevant only by introducing an element of allegory.[63] Two criticisms must be made of this latter position: (a) He has forgotten his

[61] Geraint V. Jones, *The Art and Truth of the Parables*, pp. 113, 122, 129–131, 163, 165.
[62] *Ibid.*, pp. 141–143.
[63] *Ibid.*, pp. 136, 144, 161.

own view that form gives to a work of art a certain independence of its situation of origin. (b) He has failed to grasp that implicit *in* the very pattern of connections is an understanding of existence. These two points together mean that at least those parables with aesthetic form have an understanding of existence which is not completely tied to their original setting. With respect to the parables which Jones does see as having a relevance for later times, it is not that he has interpreted the existential understanding implicit in the union of form and content, but he has rather applied a point or points of content to later circumstances. With reference to The Divided House, Jones notes that internal disunity is a problem in many areas of experience: psychological, political, and ecclesiastical. Or in discussing The Talents he points out that each servant's receiving an amount of money corresponding to his ability (Matt. 25:15) expresses a principle of wide application.[64] Jones holds, further, that the existential challenge of decision gives an underlying unity to many of the parables of whatever class,[65] but he does not relate this position clearly and consistently to his threefold classification.

According to Linnemann every attempt to seize a parable of Jesus by direct apprehension without going back to the historical situation—and this, within limits, is what the aesthetic approach does attempt—yields no more than a theological assertion or a moral demand.[66] If that yield is all that the aesthetic approach accomplished, we would have to agree with Linnemann that it is both less and other than the original meaning of Jesus' parables.[67] But the fact of the matter is that the aesthetic approach does much more than she allows, while it is the one-point, historical methodology which attenuates

[64] Cf. *ibid.*, pp. 144, 152, 153.
[65] *Ibid.*, pp. 153, 155.
[66] Linnemann, *Gleichnisse*, p. 41.
[67] Cf. *ibid.*, pp. 41–42.

the meaning of the parables by vitiating their aesthetic function.

Let us recall that language used aesthetically grasps the attention of the total psychosomatic man in a way that propositional discourse does not because in the former, content and form are more organically united and content depends more on form than in the latter case. Therefore, the parables as aesthetic objects are able to engage non-referentially the focal attention of the *whole* man upon a configuration of happening existence.[68] It is because the engagement of the attention is non-referential that the need for decision is so compelling and the possibility of a change in the structure of existence at the optimum. And the non-referential engagement of the attention depends on the interlocking, centripetally organized unity of form-and-content. The one-point, historical methodology shatters this unity, diminishes the attention grasping power of the total form, and hence reduces the power of the parable to be a language event.

In addition, the understanding of the happening existence which is implicit in the parable is implicit in the form as a whole, and to grasp this understanding is to be focally aware of the total gestalt. Therefore, to derive the meaning of the parable from one point is to shift focal attention from the whole—its proper focus—to one of the subsidiary particulars and thereby to distort the understanding.[69]

The one-point approach cannot completely destroy, of course, the parable's proper function, for the parable will work its effects to some extent despite an inappropriate hermeneutical procedure. By the same token, a more fitting method cannot completely reproduce the parable's effect, for only the parable

---

[68] I have adopted the term "happening existence" as a brief way of suggesting that in Jesus' parables, as well as in much other literature, human existence is not static but is always occurring—through dramatic encounters, the acquiring of new insights, and the gaining and losing of possibilities.

[69] Cf. Polanyi, *Man*, p. 32.

itself in its uniqueness can work its full effect. But critical interpretation can do something, and that something involves doing as much justice as possible to the particular kind of text that it is dealing with. This means that in the case of Jesus' parables, in order to be appropriate, interpretation should not isolate one point but should call attention to the total configuration, to the nature of the interconnections, and to the understanding implicitly contained therein.

The parables do point in a subsidiary way to Jesus' historical situation, and interpretation must also take this into account. They are windows to Jesus' ministry in both ways that the window analogy was used in the previous section of this chapter. The world of which they give us a new view is the world into which Jesus has come, and their inseparable connection with Jesus' ministry gives to them for the theologian-interpreter a normative value that other literary works need not have for the literary critic. At the same time it is in some measure through the parables that the Christian community sees Jesus as it does.

5. The Literary Criticism of the Parables

At this point it seems well to draw some lines together and to sum up the difference between the parables themselves and the interpretation of them. To approach this through an analogy we might say that a novel is the pre-philosophical living-through of an experience within an horizon[70] or the giving of a new configuration to pre-conceptual existential forces.[71] This pre-articulate element must be something of what Frye has in mind when he speaks of the "dumbness" of literature which calls for interpretation or criticism.[72] We have noted that in aesthetic experience focal attention is on the pattern of

[70] Novak, "Philosophy and Fiction," p. 101.
[71] Krieger, *Window*, pp. 33, 62–66.
[72] Frye, *Anatomy*, pp. 4–5, 27–28, 86.

happening existence while subsidiary attention is on the implied understanding of existence. In interpretation, on the other hand, focal attention is shifted to the subsidiary thought element which now (in interpretation) becomes focal. Thus the strictly aesthetic posture is abandoned, with the loss of an aspect of its event character, but it is abandoned for the sake of achieving conceptual clarity. In aesthetic experience the focal attention is non-referentially grasped, and the *whole* self is moved in ways of which the beholder or reader is not fully aware. At the same time, because the beholder is so fully engaged in the aesthetic object, its implied understanding of existence and the issues of a decision between understandings of existence may not be immediately apparent. It is in this connection that critical interpretation can shed light and thus enhance the language event in its own way. Interpretation cannot, however, reproduce the attention grasping power of the aesthetic object and the concomitant disposition of the whole self toward or away from the world of that object. While interpretation grows out of literature and seeks to be faithful to it, it has its own conceptual framework and structure. In order to bring what is implicit to clarity it must—in contradistinction to literature itself—use language in a propositional, referential, and discursive way.[73]

Similarly we may say that faith, as the New Testament understands it, is the relatively non-conceptual openness of man to the word of God. Yet faith is not devoid of an implicit understanding or thought element, and theology is the bringing to conceptual clarity of faith's own understanding of God, man, and the world. As such, theological thought is to some degree objectifying (cf. chap. 2, sec. 5).

Jesus' parables as aesthetic objects are new configurations of happening existence containing an implied understanding of

[73] *Ibid.*, pp. 6, 16, 27–28, 86, 89; Krieger, *Window*, pp. 62–63; Gardner, *Criticism*, p. 19.

existence, and as biblical texts they communicate to us the nature of faith and unfaith. That is to say, the understanding of existence implied in the plots—in the human encounters and their outcomes—is an understanding of existence in faith or unfaith. The parables do not teach directly or focally about God; therefore the first task is to work out the existential implications of the human interrelationships *within* the parable. But this existential understanding is then to be applied to the divine-human relationship as a definition of faith or unfaith. The latter step is indicated because inasmuch as the parables are clearly a part of Jesus' proclamation of the kingdom of God, certain figures in the parables inevitably point *subsidiarily* to God, and because the element of the surprising and the extraordinary suggests the divine dimension.

In the interpretation of the parables, then, literary criticism and theological-existential exegesis coalesce as the conceptual articulation of the nature of existence in faith or unfaith, which was configured and dramatized in the parables in a preconceptual way. Because the parables are window-mirror gestalten within larger gestalten, a comprehensive interpretation of the parables requires an articulation of the relationship of the parables to the larger complexes, that is, the Synoptic Gospels (cf. chap. 6).

Jesus' parables, of course, were first spoken and not written, and their folk or popular character has been amply demonstrated.[74] The distinctions between folk and written literature, however, are not hard and fast, and the continuity between the two levels has been recognized by literary critics.[75] My purpose now is to point out certain connections between the parables and developed literature which justify our treating the

[74] Rudolf Bultmann, *The History of the Synoptic Tradition*, pp. 188 ff.; B. T. D. Smith, *The Parables of the Synoptic Gospels*, pp. 35 ff.; Linnemann, *Gleichnisse*, pp. 21 ff.
[75] Cf. Wellek and Warren, *Literature*, p. 36; Frye, *Anatomy*, p. 104.

former as aesthetic objects. A number of features belonging to narrative fiction will be briefly discussed and a few illustrations from the parables will be given. Then those parables which manifest most or all of these features and which will be interpreted in Part Two will be mentioned. It must be shown that content and form have been brought into an organic unity which can evoke the focal attention non-referentially.

(1) Narrative fiction depicts actions and persons which belong to the world of imagination. Its relationship to the phenomenal world is potential, and the hypothetical element is basic.[76] This is also true of the parables: they are freely invented stories.

(2) In the criticism of fiction "plot" is the term for the narrative structure, which is composed of smaller narrative structures or episodes.[77] In the history of Western literature the two basic kinds of plot movement are the comic and the tragic. In comedy we have an upward movement toward well-being and the inclusion of the protagonist in a new or renewed society, while in tragedy we have a plot falling toward catastrophe and the isolation of the protagonist from society.[78] The terms "comedy" and "tragedy" are being used here in the broadest possible way of plot movement. Employed in this manner, they suggest no particular theology or philosophy but leave the way open for various theological-philosophical implications, that is, various views about how and why catastrophe or well-being occur. A play of Sophocles, for example, and a parable of Jesus may both have a tragic plot structure but different implications about how and why the movement ends in catastrophe. Thus there are different tragic views and different comic views.

In Jesus' parables these two basic plot structures are clearly

---

[76] Frye, *Anatomy*, pp. 80, 93; Wellek and Warren, *Literature*, pp. 14–15.
[77] Cf. Wellek and Warren, *Literature*, pp. 206–207.
[78] Cf. Frye, *Anatomy*, pp. 35, 162, 192.

seen in a number of cases. In The Ten Maidens all of the young ladies hopefully anticipate meeting the bridegroom and participating in the wedding feast; but as it turns out, five of them are finally excluded from the festal occasion. Thus we see a plot falling toward disappointment and isolation from a joyous society. In The Prodigal Son, on the other hand, we see an upward movement from destitution and despair to physical well-being and personal reconciliation in a renewed society.

(3) The dramatic quality of fiction and of the literature of the stage is centered in encounter—characteristically involving conflict—and in dialogue.[79] Auerbach has pointed out that the concrete dramatization of two actors face to face is not found in ancient historiography, and even the classical stage tends toward the rhetorical. But in the Bible we do find spontaneous, brief dialogue and direct discourse, which affected the later development of realism in literature.[80]

The Unjust Steward presents us with a rich employer and his estate manager in a personal encounter involving both conflict and direct discourse. Also in The Unforgiving Servant there are two scenes of face to face confrontation involving direct discourse. In The Wicked Tenants the conflict reaches the point of murder.

(4) Fictions may be classified according to the protagonist's power of action:[81] (a) He may be superior in kind to men and to their environment; thus he is a god, and we have the category of myth. (b) He may be superior in degree to other men and to their environment. The laws of nature are slightly suspended, and magic may be present. Here we have romance—legend, folk tale, and fairy story. (c) The protagonist may be superior in degree to other men but not to their environment. He is subject to criticism. This mode is designated as

[79] Wellek and Warren, Literature, pp. 206–207; Wilder, Rhetoric, p. 59.
[80] Auerbach, Mimesis, pp. 75–77; cf. also Wilder, Rhetoric, p. 54.
[81] Frye, Anatomy, pp. 33–34.

97

the high mimetic,[82] and in it we have epic and classical tragedy. (d) He is superior neither to other men nor to his environment but is rather like us. This is the low mimetic mode to which realism belongs. (e) He is inferior so that we have a sense of looking down on bondage, frustration, and absurdity. This is the ironic mode.

The characters in Jesus' parables fall in a striking and consistent way into one of these classes—the low mimetic or realistic. They are people like us who can do about what we can do. There is nothing of the mythical[83] or romantic, and the only tendency toward the high mimetic is in the few cases where a king appears as a character (The Unforgiving Servant; The Wedding Garment), but this tendency is not really carried out. On the other hand, even those characters who meet a tragic fate do not belong to the ironic mode. They do not fall into catastrophe because of external or internal determinism but because they made a choice which was not necessary.[84]

(5) The imagery or symbolism usually associated with the low mimetic mode is at the descriptive level; that is, it attempts "to give as clear and honest an impression of external reality as is possible" within the hypothetical structure of literature. The images are drawn from ordinary experience, and the organizing ideas are making and working.[85]

In the light of the foregoing the imagery of Jesus' parables is seen to be consistent with their character type. It has often been noted by New Testament scholars that the imagery of the parables on the whole is not explicitly religious but is drawn from the everyday family and business life of rural and

---

[82] For Aristotle art is the *mimēsis*—imitation—of life and action (*Poetics* 1. 4. 6).

[83] The master in The Talents takes on mythical overtones when power is attributed to him to cast men into outer darkness (Matt. 25:30), but this is hardly an original part of the parable.

[84] This point will need some modification in the later discussion.

[85] Frye, *Anatomy*, pp. 79, 116, 154.

small town Palestine.[86] C. H. Dodd demonstrates at some length the elaborated and realistic detail with which the parables present the life of a small agricultural town.[87] The working image is central, for example, in The Workers in the Vineyard and in The Talents.

When we consider Jesus' parables in connection with these features from the literary tradition—and the literary tradition has also been considered in connection with the parables—several parables emerge as clearly defined works of narrative literary art and fall into two formal classes. In the class of low mimetic, realistic tragedy we see realistic imagery and ordinary people in dramatic encounters and conflicts moving downward toward catastrophe. Here we have The Talents, The Ten Maidens, The Wedding Garment, The Wicked Tenants, and The Unforgiving Servant.[88] In the class of low mimetic, realistic comedy we view realistic imagery and ordinary people in dramatic, face-to-face confrontations moving upward toward well-being. Here we have The Workers in the Vineyard, The Unjust Steward, and The Prodigal Son. Since these parables have an identifiable form, they should be treated as aesthetic objects. And one of the main reasons for approaching them first from the standpoint of their understanding of human existence and then seeing the divine impingement as an implication of this understanding of existence is that in none of these parables is

[86] Cf. Joachim Jeremias, The Parables of Jesus, p. 11; Jones, Parables, pp. 112–113; Ernst Fuchs, Studies of the Historical Jesus, p. 73; "The New Testament and the Hermeneutical Problem," in The New Hermeneutic, p. 126; J. Alexander Findlay, Jesus and His Parables (London: The Religious Book Club, 1951), preface; Wilder, Rhetoric, p. 81.

[87] C. H. Dodd, The Authority of the Bible (London: Nisbet, 1948), pp. 148–152.

[88] In view of the prominence of the tragic motif, it is strange that Findlay should claim Jesus' support for his own view that man's basic nature is good, if not divine, and that the "debunking" novels are in error. Cf. Findlay, Parables, pp. 130–131, 137, 141–142. Findlay seems to assume that because Jesus used ordinary, human, non-religious imagery he automatically considered man basically good or divine.

the formal shape determined by the figure that points subsidiarily to God. Rather in every case the form is determined by the story of a very human character, or characters. For example, in The Talents the formal shape of the story is determined, not by the employer, but by what happens to the one-talent man.

In the parables which we will consider, the plot, on the whole, is the controlling form to which all else is related.[89] This is not surprising in view of the fact that for the Bible in general the basic speech-mode is the story—a narration of action in time—and this fact suggests that in the biblical view life itself is of the nature of a dramatic plot. Other religions, of course, have used stories, but "the narrative mode is uniquely important in Christianity."[90]

The primacy of plot in the parables makes the Aristotelian literary approach especially pertinent, for the heart of Aristotle's famous definition of tragedy is that it is the imitation of a serious action. Therefore, of the six parts of a tragedy—plot, characters, diction, thought, spectacle, and melody—the most important is plot, the combination of the incidents.[91] This point of view has been taken up by the "neo-Aristotelians" who have argued that imagery and other elements receive their meaning from their place in the plot.[92]

Our emphasis on plot, however, should not make us forget that all narrative literature contains both plot and theme or thought in some relationship. In fact they are two sides of the same formal principle with plot being theme in movement

[89] Cf. Frye, Anatomy, pp. 82–83.
[90] Wilder, Rhetoric, pp. 20, 37–38, 64, 78–79; Samuel Laeuchli, The Language of Faith, p. 232.
[91] Aristotle Poetics 6; cf. Wheelwright, Fountain, p. 188.
[92] W. R. Keast, "The 'New Criticism' and King Lear," in Critics and Criticism, ed. R. S. Crane (Chicago: University of Chicago Press, 1952), pp. 120–121; Elder Olson, "William Empson, Contemporary Criticism, and Poetic Diction," in Critics and Criticism, p. 54.

and theme being plot at a standstill. In some works plot is more important, while in others theme is, but the decision about which one is more prominent will often be a matter of interpretive emphasis. Of plot we ask "How will it turn out?" and of theme "What is the point?"[93] Of the eight parables which we will consider it seems probable that plot is somewhat more prominent in The Unjust Steward, The Ten Maidens, The Talents, The Wedding Garment, and The Wicked Tenants, while in The Prodigal Son, The Workers in the Vineyard, and The Unforgiving Servant, theme is perhaps more prominent. We may bring together our existential (thematic) and aesthetic concerns by stating that the ontological possibility—possibility in principle—of losing existence is aesthetically the tragic movement, and the ontological possibility of gaining existence is aesthetically the comic movement. How either one occurs ontically—actually or concretely—is seen in the nature of the connections between events—as whether one episode follows another through the exercise of freedom or by being determined—and in the thought and self-understanding of the characters. Since a parable as an aesthetic object is within limits an autonomous world, the gain or loss of the one opportunity which is presented in the parable suggests the gain or loss of existence itself.

The organic unity of form and content may be briefly demonstrated by a look at The Talents. In the beginning of the story an employer called together three servants to each of whom he gave an amount of money, and in this first part of the story we see how they handled what had been given to them. In the middle part the master returned and required the three servants to give an account of their behavior. Here the emphasis is on the one-talent man, who explained his earlier behavior and thereby gave expression to his understanding of existence.

[93] Frye, *Anatomy*, pp. 52–53, 82–83: Wellek and Warren, *Literature*, p. 208.

In the conclusion the consequence of parts one and two are drawn out. A man who behaves and thinks as the one-talent man loses all. Thus we have a beginning, middle, and end interlocked within a plot moving downward from well-being to loss.

At this point we might elaborate somewhat on the existential implications of plot structure by considering the critical methodology worked out by Preston Roberts. Roberts asks certain pertinent questions of the plot (the direction of its movement, the content of the recognition scene, the object of the character's accusations, the nature of the protagonist's flaw, the implications of the ending, the presence or absence of freedom and openness),[94] and because these questions are variously answered in different works, we are able to see different understandings of the possibilities of human existence. In Roberts' approach our grasp of a work's existential understanding grows out of being attentive to the interrelationships of the elements within the aesthetic object and not out of speculations about the author's original theological intentions nor out of any allegorical pointing outward in the story. Working in this way Roberts has identified three different motifs, each combining plot and symbolism in a unity, which present three different views of what man's possibilities are. We may summarize:

(a) The tragic (classical) image of man is that of a noble figure flawed by finite ignorance and/or hybris moving without freedom from good to bad fortune and to an end "after which there is nothing." In his recognition scene he comes to the bitter knowledge that he has accomplished the opposite of his intentions, and "he accuses the very character of life and history" or his own unalterable essence.[95]

[94] Preston Roberts, "A Christian Theory of Dramatic Tragedy," *Journal of Religion*, 31 (1951), 8, 10–12, 14–16; "Bringing Pathos into Focus," *Motive*, 14 (December, 1953), 9–10.

[95] Roberts, "Tragedy," pp. 10–11, 14–17, 20; "Pathos," p. 10.

(b) The modern image of man is that of a more or less abnormal figure—a victim of psychological, sociological, or cosmic forces—moving without freedom from a bad to a worse situation and to an end after which there is nothing. In the recognition scene—if he is capable of recognizing anything— he is aware of the loneliness and misery of his life and accuses the nature of life and history.[96]

(c) The Christian image of man is that of a more or less normal figure flawed by idolatry and pretension moving with limited but real freedom from a bad to a good situation and to an ending which is a new beginning, even if it is life found in death. In the recognition scene he is aware of guilt, judgment and forgiveness and accuses himself, but a contingent, forgivable self, not an unalterable essence.[97]

Roberts' approach will be helpful in interpreting the parables; and the parables in turn are illuminating models for a literary representation of the Christian view of man, models which may suggest (in Part Two) certain modifications of Roberts' view of the Christian motif. The contrasts with the classical and modern motifs will also help to clarify the Christian motif. It should be noticed here that what Roberts sets forth as the Christian motif is really a comic or redemptive movement, and it has been strongly urged by others that a Christian literary representation should present a resolution of man's existential predicament.[98] Jesus' tragic parables show, however, that the New Testament may present as a self-contained and independent work just the tragic possibility which the Christian understanding of existence holds out. But the reasons for the movement to catastrophe will be different from those in Greek tragedy or modern pathos. It *is* true, more-

---

[96] Roberts, "Tragedy," p. 14; "Pathos," pp. 8–9.
[97] Roberts, "Tragedy," pp. 10–12, 16–17; "Pathos," p. 10.
[98] William V. Spanos, "Christian Drama and the Contemporary Religious Consciousness," *The Christian Scholar*, 46 (1963), 320.

over, that the full Christian story is a comedy, but a comedy in which tragedy is included and overcome, as we see in The Prodigal Son.

In concluding this section we may give somewhat more attention than we have to the theological significance of the realistic imagery in Jesus' parables. The very fact that Jesus compared the kingdom of God to ordinary, everyday people and activities suggests some kind of analogy between God and man.[99] But in view of the problems which we noticed in chapter 2 connected with describing God, Dodd is probably going too far when he states that the realism of the parables suggests, not a "mere analogy," but "an inward affinity" between the spiritual order and daily life, with nature and super-nature being one order.[100] No figure or action in the parables tells us literally what God is like, but the parables do tell us that God meets us and we are put in touch with him in the everyday and that when we respond to him our existence is structured like that of the prodigal son and not like that of the unforgiving servant. In the parables "God and the world come together"[101] showing life in the world to be meaningful. Novak has remarked that realities like water, fire, sun, earth, love, and hate seldom fall within our horizons any more; we are too preoccupied with our hour-by-hour schedules.[102] It is just such images as these, however, which meet us in the parables. We confront the love of the prodigal's father and the hatred of the wicked tenants. Vineyard owners know what the earth is like as does an unscrupulous steward who was too weak to dig. The burning heat of the day bears down on vineyard workers, but burning lamps light the festive way of a bridegroom.

[99] A. M. Hunter, *Interpreting the Parables*, pp. 15–17.
[100] C. H. Dodd, *The Parables of the Kingdom*, p. 10; cf. also A. T. Cadoux, *The Parables of Jesus*, p. 57.
[101] Cf. Gerhard Ebeling, *Word and Faith*, p. 356.
[102] Novak, "Philosophy and Fiction," p. 102.

These images, placed in their new configurations of meaning, call us out of our chronological preoccupations.

The impingement of the divine upon the human is indicated not only by the fact that Jesus compared the kingdom of God to ordinary happenings, but—even more importantly for our purposes—by the way everyday reality is dealt with in the parables themselves. Auerbach has shown that in the literature of antiquity outside of the Bible, everyday reality is treated in a light, comic mode but not seriously or tragically. In the Bible, on the other hand, ordinary and everyday reality is mingled with the problematic and tragic. Auerbach, furthermore, sees the Bible's rejection of the separation between the everyday and the serious as being based on the principle of the incarnation: God became incarnate in a human being of most humble origin. "The story of Christ with its ruthless mixture of everyday reality" with high and "sublime tragedy" broke the classical rule of style.[103]

The parables manifest this incarnational principle—this serious treatment of the everyday—by combining the realistic with the extraordinary and improbable. The behavior of the prodigal's father and of the vineyard owner is not what we would expect under the circumstances; the debt which the unforgiving servant owed was fantastic, and the commending of the dishonest steward surprises us; it is strange that a father would send his son to collect rent after his servants had been maltreated by the tenants, and it seems unnecessarily harsh for the bridegroom to have shut out the tardy maidens.[104] Such features burst the limits of the probable but are kept locked into the narrative frame and hence are rendered possible and

[103] Auerbach, *Mimesis*, pp. 19, 26–27, 29, 36–39, 131–136, 489–490. Spanos ("Christian Drama," pp. 319–320) suggests that contemporary Christian drama should be based on the principle of the incarnation.

[104] Cf. Jeremias, *Parables*, p. 30; Linnemann, *Gleichnisse*, p. 36; Jones, *Parables*, p. 116.

105

convincing.[105] As Wilder[106] has pointed out, this element of the extraordinary echoes the eschatological crisis note of Jesus' preaching. But it is not that such features as the one-talent man's loss of his talent, the shutting out of the foolish maidens, and the imprisonment of the unforgiving servant are allegorical pointers to the final judgment. Rather the understanding of existence implicit in eschatology[107] has been given a new and different configuration in the parables.

In view of the above one hesitates before the unconscious allegorizing which says directly that the hearer of Jesus' parables may relate himself to God as the prodigal does to his father or the late laborers do to the vineyard owner.[108] This position tends to suggest that the father or vineyard owner (allegorically) *is* God. It seems closer to the standpoint of the parables themselves to say that the element of the extraordinary does not point directly to God, but being fused into the story—into the aesthetic mingling of the realistic and the surprising—it suggests that everyday existence is crossed by the problematical, contingent, and unpredictable. This in turn does suggest indirectly an openness of existence to the transcendent,[109] and it is in this way that eschatological awareness would be represented *within* the aesthetic. The parables' existential understanding is that existence is gained or lost in the midst of ordinary life, that the eschatological occurs within the everyday.[110] It should be remembered that the parables also

[105] Cf. Linnemann, *Gleichnisse*, pp. 20, 36.

[106] *Rhetoric*, pp. 82–85.

[107] Cf. Rudolf Bultmann, "Man between the Times According to the New Testament," pp. 248–266.

[108] Fuchs, *Historical Jesus*, p. 221.

[109] The parables turn out to be different from most low mimetic realistic literature, in which the divine has little place. Cf. Frye, *Anatomy*, p. 154.

[110] This intermingling of the everyday with the eschatological opposes the dichotomy Bonhoeffer saw between the existentialist theology of the boundary situation and the theology of God in the midst of life. Cf. Dietrich Bonhoeffer, *Letters and Papers from Prison*, ed. E. Bethge, trans. R. H. Fuller

give our understanding of God some positive content in the sense indicated in chapter 2 (cf. pp. 64–66).

As a kind of epilogue to this chapter, I find it hard to agree with the position of John Killinger that an artist may not serve Christianity in the *highest* fashion. "No man existentially concerned with last things," he says, would give his time to building a cathedral or writing a *Commedia*.[111] Killinger seems to presuppose that Christian faith is something separable from life which can and should be pursued in independence of other things. This would entail holding that no vocation except the professional ministry can serve Christianity in the *highest* way. If, on the other hand, Christian faith is a way of living and understanding life in this world as given by God, and if last things are the existential crises of everyday life, then the artist's vocation may be as highly Christian as any other and he may be quite eschatologically involved. Jesus must have had to give some time to the creation of the parables.

(New York: Macmillan Paperbacks, 1962), pp. 113, 165–166, 190–191, 195–197.

[111] John Killinger, *The Failure of Theology in Modern Literature* (New York: Abingdon Press, 1963), pp. 223–224. In fairness to Killinger it should be said that he does consider art very significant.

PART TWO

INTERPRETIVE

4

The Tragic Parables

We should remind ourselves that the category of tragedy is being used in the broad sense of a plot moving downward toward catastrophe and the isolation of the protagonist. From this standpoint certain of the parables may be called tragic. These parables also share with tragedy in general a thematic attentiveness to the insecurities and contingencies of life[1] and to the question of what it means to be when one is in a boundary situation.[2] As one turns, however, to the why and how of catastrophe and insecurity and to the question of the content of human existence, certain significant differences between Jesus' tragic parables and other tragedies may be noted.

While human freedom is not absent from classical tragedy,[3] the emphasis is on fate, a fate that is stronger than the gods;[4] that is, man's lot is often determined by external forces having no moral implications.[5] Divine interventions, oracles, or family curses are able to initiate and direct action.[6] In the opinion of Oscar Mandel the *inevitability* of suffering is the

[1] Cf. Nathan A. Scott, Jr. (ed.), *The Tragic Vision and the Christian Faith* (New York: Association Press, 1957), p. x.

[2] Richard B. Sewall, *The Vision of Tragedy* (New Haven and London: Yale University Press, paperback ed., 1962), p. 5.

[3] *Ibid.*, p. 45; William C. Greene, *Moira* (New York: Harper Torchbooks, 1963), p. 91.

[4] Northrop Frye, *Anatomy of Criticism*, p. 208; Sewall, *Tragedy*, p. 45.

[5] Greene, *Moira*, p. 90.

[6] *Ibid.*

very kernel of the definition of tragedy. In the tragic vision there is a necessary and inescapable fatal defect in the relationship between an undertaken purpose and the protagonist's world. What he attempts inevitably leads to suffering.[7]

In Jesus' tragic parables freedom is much more apparent. We do not find action being instigated and determined by such factors as divine oracles and family curses. Yet the note of inevitability is present. Man is free to act in various ways but not to avoid the consequences. One cannot have a certain understanding of existence and act upon it without meeting catastrophe, that is, losing his existence; but one need not have that understanding of existence. In the five parables which we will consider a particular course of action is inexorably followed by a downfall. The grounding of this inevitability, however, is not the same as in classical and certain other tragedy.

The tragic hero of the literary tradition—especially in classical tragedy—initiates and pursues a course of action that has a certain seriousness or magnitude. He answers the call of honor regardless of the consequences, pursuing his purpose in the face of every obstacle and acting in the interest of what he regards as most authentic about himself.[8] That the tragic hero suffers or dies matters little since he saves his authentic self by refusing to sink into second-hand morality.[9] What man is found capable of at the boundary situation is the truth of tragedy.[10]

The purposeful action of the tragic hero must be seen

[7] Oscar Mandel, A Definition of Tragedy (New York University Press, 1961), pp. 20, 23, 24.
[8] Cf. Mandel, Tragedy, p. 20; Greene, Moira, p. 91; Gilbert Norwood, Greek Tragedy (Dramabooks ed.; New York: Hill and Wang, n.d.), p. 178; Nathan A. Scott, Jr., "The Bias of Comedy and the Narrow Escape into Faith," The Christian Scholar, 44 (1961), 17.
[9] Norwood, Tragedy, p. 178.
[10] Sewall, Tragedy, p. 7.

111

against its ultimate backdrop. There is in the tragic view a balanced cosmic order made up of neutral parts so that no one element should be elevated: "the truth is in the whole."[11] The human protagonist, with his finite limitations and his involvement in the world of action, cannot see the whole and, therefore, acts to affirm a part of it as he relentlessly pursues his purpose. Thus his finite ignorance and mistaken judgment engender hybris—a challenge to the balanced order. Hybris, however, is not "sin." It is not that his pursuit is in itself wrong but rather that in elevating one part of the neutral order he is causing an imbalance. Without hybris, however, there would be no significant action. The order reacts to balance itself once more—perhaps through human actions, perhaps through nature—and the hero is crushed. The rebalancing of the cosmic order may or may not coincide with moral "justice."[12]

When we look at Jesus' tragic parables, we would not, I think, say that the protagonists are moved by purposes of a certain seriousness or magnitude. Their actions are quite everyday in character. Nor are Jesus' characters intentioned by the call of honor come what may; they act, rather, to preserve their safety, to secure a simple pleasure, or to obtain a benefit for themselves whatever the cost to others. The deeds of the parabolic characters are not neutral acts of unbalancing the order of the universe but are rather wrong or evil in the light of norms held by another character or found implicitly in the telling of the story. The protagonist's downfall comes because the character whose norms he has violated has the power to dispose of him and personally reacts to do so. As we

[11] Cf. H. D. F. Kitto, *Greek Tragedy* (rev. ed.; Garden City, New York: Doubleday Anchor Books, 1954), pp. 151–153; Edmond La B. Cherbonnier, "Biblical Faith and the Idea of Tragedy," in *The Tragic Vision and the Christian Faith*, p. 26.

[12] Cf. Kitto, *Tragedy*, pp. 151–153; Cherbonnier, "Tragedy," p. 27; Greene, *Moira*, p. 93; Sewall, *Tragedy*, pp. 35–37.

noticed in chapter 3, the characters who have the power of disposal point subsidiarily to God; thus the human interrelationships in the parables point indirectly to possible divine-human relationships and to the nature of sin and judgment. To lose one's true existence and to experience the judgment of God are two sides of the same reality, and it is the loss of existence, rather than a demonstration of the greatness that man is capable of in boundary situations, which appears in the tragic parables. We see then that some of the characteristic motifs of tragedy are modified in Jesus' tragic parables both by their everyday realism and by the influence of the biblical understanding of sin.

In concluding this introductory section we may note that if typically modern tragedy is informed by a sense of the death of God,[13] Jesus' tragic parables are sharply different in that existential extinction is a possibility precisely because of God and his judgment.

1. The Talents (Matt. 25:14-30)

14 For it will be as when a man going on a journey called his servants and entrusted to them his property; 15to one he gave five talents, to another two, to another one, to each according to his ability. Then he went away. 16He who had received the five talents went at once and traded with them; and he made five talents more. 17So also, he who had the two talents made two talents more. 18But he who had received the one talent went and dug in the ground and hid his master's money. 19Now after a long time the master of those servants came and settled accounts with them. 20And he who had received the five talents came forward, bringing five talents more, saying, "Master, you delivered to me five talents; here I have made five talents more." 21His master said to him, "Well done, good and faithful servant; you have been faithful over a little, I will set you over much; enter into the joy of your master." 22And he also who had the two talents came for-

13 Cf. Scott, "Comedy," pp. 10–12.

ward, saying, "Master, you delivered to me two talents; here I have made two talents more." [23]His master said to him, "Well done, good and faithful servant; you have been faithful over a little, I will set you over much; enter into the joy of your master." [24]He also who had received the one talent came forward, saying, "Master, I knew you to be a hard man, reaping where you did not sow, and gathering where you did not winnow; [25]so I was afraid, and I went and hid your talent in the ground. Here you have what is yours." [26]But his master answered him, "You wicked and slothful servant! You knew that I reap where I have not sowed, and gather where I have not winnowed? [27]Then you ought to have invested my money with the bankers, and at my coming I should have received what was my own with interest. [28]So take the talent from him, and give it to him who has the ten talents. [29]For to every one who has will more be given, and he will have abundance; but from him who has not, even what he has will be taken away. [30]And cast the worthless servant into the outer darkness; there men will weep and gnash their teeth."

(1) *Historico-literary criticism.* While The Talents in Matthew shows fewer allegorical additions than Luke's The Pounds, Luke's parable may be more original on the point of the amount of money (cf. Matt. 25:15; Luke 19:13);[14] and The Talents does reveal some secondary features. Matt. 25:30 is a favorite—and peculiarly—Matthean saying (cf. 8:12; 22:13) which turns the master of the parable into the eschatological judge. It is not original here, nor is it a saying of Jesus at all. Also the "enter into the joy of your Lord" (25:21, 23) appears to be an allegorical addition with both christological and eschatological overtones.

Matt. 25:29 was a free-floating saying (cf. Mark 4:25; Matt. 13:12; Luke 8:18) and is scarcely original here. Against those who deny the genuineness of Matt. 25:28,[15] however, it should be said that 25:29—which applies the point in 25:28 rather

---

[14] Joachim Jeremias, *The Parables of Jesus*, pp. 27–28.
[15] As A. T. Cadoux, *The Parables of Jesus*, pp. 67–68; B. T. D. Smith, *The Parables of the Synoptic Gospels*, p. 167.

than interpreting the thought of the parable as a whole—would hardly have been added had not 25:28 already been there. Nor will Cadoux's point stand that the one-talent man had already given his allotted funds back in 25:25, making 25:28 therefore superfluous.[16] The answers of the five- and two-talent men (25:20, 22) are essentially the same in form as that of the one-talent man, but there is no indication that they were giving up their allotment. The one-talent man in 25:25 is simply reporting that he had kept his money safely. Jeremias regards 25:28 as an original part of the parable but as of secondary importance.[17] But it must be said that it is secondary only from the standpoint of the severely historical approach. For the aesthetic approach it is indispensable as a means of giving the narrative form its rounded completeness, of revealing the consequences of the one-talent man's action and understanding. The logic of what has gone before both calls for it and makes it important.

The context in which Matthew places the parable, as well as his addition of 25:30, shows that for him it is a Parousia parable. For Jesus, too, it had an eschatological import,[18] but in the sense indicated in chapter 3, not by pointing directly and allegorically to the final judgment. It is probable that Jesus had in mind in telling this parable those Jews—or the scribes in particular—who held fast to the law and excluded from their concern the outsiders, thus failing to be good stewards of their covenant heritage.[19] But what is the understanding of existence contained in the parable and attributed to those Jews by the fact that the one-talent man points subsidiarily to them?

(2) *Literary-existential analysis.* As we have already noted

[16] Cadoux, *Parables*, p. 68.
[17] Jeremias, *Parables*, p. 62.
[18] Cf. *ibid.*, pp. 63, 166.
[19] Cf. Cadoux, *Parables*, pp. 106, 107; C. H. Dodd, *The Parables of the Kingdom*, pp. 117–119; Smith, *Parables*, p. 168; Jeremias, *Parables*, p. 62.

(chapter 3) the tragic shape of the plot of the parable derives from the experience of the one-talent man. He began as a free man, for no external factors and no internal force beyond his own will compelled him to hide his talent in the ground while the other two men traded with their money. He could have done otherwise. It was *his* decision to understand himself in the world as he did and to act upon his understanding. But the very movement of the plot to catastrophe means that one cannot think and act as he did without losing his existence, that is, without being inauthentic or existentially dead. If the outcome of such an understanding is ultimately the death of the self, then death is implicit in it from the beginning. To grasp the content of his understanding we must turn to the recognition scene in the middle part of the parable. But some consideration of the significance of the recognition scene itself is first called for.

By recognition is meant the enlightenment of the protagonist with regard to the true nature of his actions at the moment of catastrophe.[20] As Mandel has pointed out, there are three possibilities with regard to the relationship of recognition to the story as a whole: (a) The protagonist may be lucid throughout. He knows what to expect and is not surprised by his misery. (b) He may have the hope of success and be unaware of the disaster that his purpose entails. This is true recognition tragedy, for here the protagonist recognizes the painful truth only when it is too late. (c) The protagonist proceeds and suffers in ignorance.[21]

Jesus' parables on the whole belong to the second type. The protagonist is not expecting catastrophe and realizes after it is too late that his downfall is now inescapable. Thus it is a formal principle of Jesus' parables that the recognition scene occurs characteristically between the initiating or tragic action of

[20] Cf. Mandel, *Tragedy*, p. 148.
[21] *Ibid.*

116

the protagonist and his downfall. The recognition, however, may be only implicit or may hardly be present at all (as in The Wicked Tenants) in which case the parable gravitates toward the third category above. Here it needs to be pointed out that these formal aspects have an existential implication which inclines one to modify a distinction which Preston Roberts has drawn between the Greek-tragic and Christian literary motifs. According to Roberts the recognition scene in Greek tragedy is likely to be after the tragic deed because such tragedy is born of finite ignorance and erring judgment.[22] In the case of the Christian hero, on the other hand, the chief problem is not knowledge. He sees some alternatives as clearly good and some as clearly evil. The choices are not ambiguous; therefore, in the Christian story the recognition scene characteristically comes before the tragic deed.[23]

As we have noticed, Roberts' position is not borne out, at least, in the case of Jesus' parables. It is true that the chief problem of Jesus' protagonists is not finite ignorance, but it is not true that they see their alternatives clearly and unambiguously as good or evil. The very fact that the parabolic characters see the folly and self-destructiveness of their deeds—when they do in fact see these things—only *after* they have acted shows that their actions were infused with blindness. This formal-existential theme is paralleled in Jesus' non-parabolic teaching. The perversity of the men of Jesus' generation is epitomized in their inability to perceive the significance of their own time (Luke 12:54-57; Matt. 16:1-4). It would not be fair to blame them if what they lacked was intellectual knowledge or information. But their imperception or blindness is reprehensible and blameworthy because it is a lack of that awareness which is given with existence itself when the latter is

[22] Preston Roberts, "A Christian Theory of Dramatic Tragedy," pp. 10, 16.
[23] *Ibid.*, pp. 12, 16.

turned in the right direction. That is, they are considered capable of responding to Jesus' presence and word. Their blindness is grounded in a self-deception which has come to believe its own lies and therefore cannot recognize what is true and right. What is really darkness is taken to be light (Matt. 6:22-23; Luke 11:34-35). With the question of what understanding of existence produces such blindness we return to The Talents.

In the recognition scene we have face to face confrontation, direct discourse, and conflict in the case of the master and the one-talent man. The latter explained to his master why he hid his talent in the ground. Part of his explanation turns out to be the real reason, though not a good reason, for the hiding, while another part of his reason was rejected by the master as untrue. Our protagonist had some dim awareness of why he had acted as he had, but he did not through his own resources recognize the evil and folly of it. He was informed of the latter by his master after it was too late for him to do anything about it.

The one-talent man stated that because he knew his master to be a hard man, reaping where he had not sown, he was afraid and therefore hid his talent. Then he showed his master that he had preserved what was his. The master replied that if his servant really had known him to be a hard and scheming man he would have invested his money for the earning of interest. The one-talent man had not acted on what he claimed was his reason, thus it must not have been his real reason. The fact remains, however, that he was afraid. Therefore, he acted to preserve his safety. Or to be more precise, he acted as little as possible. He sought to avoid the risk of trading in the market and expected to stay at least minimally in his master's good graces by preserving exactly what had been entrusted to him. He hoped for a safe bargain. In the fear of the one-talent man we see the anxiety of one who will not step into the unknown. He will not risk trying to fulfill his own possibilities; therefore,

118

his existence is circumscribed in the narrowest kind of way. Action is paralyzed by anxiety, and the self of our protagonist is only a shadow of what it potentially is.

Although the one-talent man hoped to retain the favor of his master, he revealed an obscure and inchoate sense of guilt which is seen in the fact that he accused his master of hardness and thus tried to make the latter responsible for his own failure. Moreover, his verbal expression of fear and his refusal to risk action are an implicit accusation against life itself. They show that he viewed the universe as inimical to the human enterprise and saw self-defensive non-action, therefore, as the appropriate course to take in life.

The servant's breach of trust in failing to do business with his master's goods[24] is grounded in his existential flaw. He started as a free man, but he refused to be responsible. That is, when he faced the crisis of having to give an account of his actions, he placed the blame for his failure on someone and something other than himself. In refusing to hold himself accountable he understood himself as a victim, and in understanding himself as a victim he *was* a victim, unable to act significantly. The master, by rejecting the charge that he (the master) was a hard man, forced the servant to see—at least by implication—that he himself (the servant) was responsible. The servant was paralyzed, not because he was in a victimizing context, but because he chose to understand himself as a victim. By that time, however, it was too late to act differently because the talent was to be taken from him. We see the following connected movement: *from* the refusal to take a risk, *through* repressed guilt which is projected onto someone else, *to* the loss of the opportunity for meaningful existence. The refusal to take a risk results in an inability to hold oneself accountable, but it is also grounded in a sense of the universe

[24] Cf. Dodd, *Parables*, p. 118; Wilhelm Michaelis, *Die Gleichnisse Jesu*, pp. 107–108.

as hostile. The circle is vicious. The man whose primary concern was to avoid risk and to be safe was forced to recognize that self-protective non-action is not after all the way to well-being.

The ending—the clear implication that the talent is to be taken from him (25:28)—is something after which there is nothing. The autonomy of the aesthetic object prevents our speculating about what further opportunities he might have had, and the existential implication of this is that the one-talent man's understanding of existence is non-existence. Smith holds, as a part of his view that 25:28 is not genuine, that the one-talent man would actually have been glad to be rid of his responsibility.[25] But Michaelis is right that his being no longer able to administer the talent is a punishment.[26] The one-talent man himself, from what we learn of him, may well have been glad to be free of his responsibility; but the meaning of a work of narrative art is not exhausted by the perspective of one or all of the characters. From the standpoint of the story as a whole, the being rid of his responsibility is at the same time the loss of opportunity, of possibility, of a place to exist meaningfully in the world.

(3) *Existential-theological interpretation.* When the parable's understanding of existence is seen as a pointer to the divine-human relationship, the refusal to risk and the concomitant inability to hold oneself responsible become unfaith. The man who retreats from risking his life wants to provide his own security, whether it be in material goods (Matt. 6:25-34; Luke 12:16-20) or in a sense of religious achievement (Luke 18:10-14). Such seeking for security is death, for in it one becomes the slave of the very realities which he hopes will give him security. To know on the other hand, that one is sus-

[25] Smith, *Parables*, p. 167.
[26] Michaelis, *Gleichnisse*, p. 110.

tained by a transcendent and unprovable ground—even if that sustenance is only the awareness that one really exists—is to be able to risk one's security (Matt. 6:25-34). And such risking is life, for in it one is free from the anxious effort to provide one's own security through the world, and in such freedom life in the world is good. Moreover, the man who can risk can hold himself responsible, for in those moments when he knows himself as called to account he also knows himself as forgiven (Matt. 18:23-27).

Actually the effort to make oneself secure by avoiding risk and by striking a bargain with God is a delusion (Luke 12:20; 18:14). It is the self-deceiving attempt which both is and engenders that blindness which prevents one from understanding his time and from grasping the folly of his own actions.

With regard to the understanding of time in The Talents, the reference to the "long time" which the master was gone may well for Matthew have become a statement of the delay of the Parousia. But if Matthew added the note that the time was *long*, the original parable still required an indication of some passage of time. For if the three servants are to be held accountable, they must have sufficient time to perform those acts for which they will be held responsible. Thus the very fact that there is an event expected in the future—the master's return—and that it is to be an accounting marks off a real present and gives the latter its character: the present is a time for risky action. The one-talent man by retreating from such a present lost his time altogether; that is, he lost the opportunity to engage himself in what constitutes the present. The chronological ending of his time of opportunity confirmed the inauthenticity of his selfhood which we have noticed. We may say then that the tragic narrative form—the plot moving to catastrophe—and the existential content—a particular understanding of inauthenticity—inhere in each other. This very inherence in

121

Jesus' parables suggests that one does not lose—or gain—his existence as an isolated individual but only within the dynamics of temporal, human relationships.

When we look at the world through the window of the understanding of existence in The Talents, we will have to say that the man who so understands himself that he seeks to avoid risky action rather than trusting God for the well-being of his existence, though he may live long chronologically, will have no present. His time will be evacuated of content.

2. The Ten Maidens (Matt. 25:1-13)

[1]Then the kingdom of heaven shall be compared to ten maidens who took their lamps and went to meet the bridegroom. [2]Five of them were foolish, and five were wise. [3]For when the foolish took their lamps, they took no oil with them; [4]but the wise took flasks of oil with their lamps. [5]As the bridegroom was delayed, they all slumbered and slept. [6]But at midnight there was a cry, "Behold, the bridegroom! Come out to meet him." [7]Then all those maidens rose and trimmed their lamps. [8]And the foolish said to the wise, "Give us some of your oil, for our lamps are going out." [9]But the wise replied, "Perhaps there will not be enough for us and for you; go rather to the dealers and buy for yourselves." [10]And while they went to buy, the bridegroom came, and those who were ready went in with him to the marriage feast; and the door was shut. [11]Afterward the other maidens came also, saying, "Lord, lord, open to us." [12]But he replied, "Truly, I say to you, I do not know you." [13]Watch therefore, for you know neither the day nor the hour.

(1) *Historico-literary criticism.* It has been claimed that in this parable Jesus himself proclaimed his coming Parousia,[27] but again it must be held that its aesthetic nature prevents such direct allegorical pointing. On the other hand, it has been claimed that it is too heavily overlaid with Christian motifs

[27] Cf. J. Arthur Baird, *The Justice of God in the Teaching of Jesus*, pp. 105–106, 129–131; Michaelis, *Gleichnisse*, pp. 92–94; W. O. E. Oesterley, *The Gospel Parables in the Light of Their Jewish Background*, p. 136.

to allow the detection of Jesus' original version, if there was one.[28] Or it has been held that The Ten Maidens was created altogether by the church in order to teach that the Parousia will not occur for a long time. Eta Linnemann,[29] who takes the latter position, denies, however, that the parable is an allegory. Yet her interpretation turns it into one, for she sees the structure of the parable as determined in detail by the eschatological problems of the post-apostolic church. She does not so much look for the existential meaning of the parable itself in its own terms as give the allegorical interpretation which Matthew undoubtedly read into it.

Because the parable makes internal sense apart from Matthew's allegorical interpretation, there seems to be no overpowering reason to deny that it was older than Matthew, and genuine. As for Matthew, he would have seen in the parable the waiting church (the maidens), the postponement of the Parousia (25:5), the unexpected occurrence of the Parousia (25:6; cf. 24:44,50), and the final judgment (25:11-12).[30] The warning to be watchful (25:13), a later addition to the parable, is not altogether appropriate inasmuch as all of the maidens went to sleep. Moreover, 25:11b-12 appears to be secondary in wording. Jesus himself seems to have used *amēn* in a unique way[31] but apparently did not put it in the mouth of his parabolic characters (cf. Matt. 18:13; Luke 11:8; 12:37; 14:24; 18:14). The double use of *kyrie* and the "I do not know you" are reminiscent of Matt. 7:22-23 and Luke 13:25-27, both of which contain elements of doubtful authenticity. We

[28] Rudolf Bultmann, *The History of the Synoptic Tradition*, pp. 119, 151, 176, 205; cf. also T. W. Manson, *The Sayings of Jesus* (London: SCM Press, 1950), pp. 243–245.

[29] *Die Gleichnisse Jesu*, pp. 132–133.

[30] Cf. Jeremias, *Parables*, p. 51.

[31] Michaelis, *Gleichnisse*, p. 92; Gerhard Ebeling, *Word and Faith*, pp. 237–238.

might conjecture that Matt. 25:11b-12 originally read something like this: "Sir, open to us." But he replied, "I tell you, I will not."

The question of the exact relationship of the parable to the wedding customs of Jesus' day remains unresolved.[32] In view of our imprecise knowledge of Palestinian wedding practices, it may be best to suppose that no one established usage is in view in the parable but that various possible wedding customs have been brought together to serve the narrative purpose of Jesus.[33]

(2) *Literary-existential analysis*. The tragic shape of the narrative is determined by the experience of the five foolish maidens. The beginning relates that ten maidens, differing sharply in wisdom, went out to meet the bridegroom. This is one of the few cases in Jesus' parables (cf. also Luke 18:6) where a figure is characterized directly by the narrator's use of an adjective—"wise" and "foolish"—rather than by simply relating his deeds and words.[34] The middle part of the story dramatizes the issue of the one group's folly. Here we learn that the groom has been delayed and that all of the maidens have gone to sleep. Then they awake to the announcement of the groom's approach, the foolish ones discovering that they are about out of oil. Being unable to find an easy solution to their problem, they go in search of oil from a merchant. While they are gone, the groom comes and the festivities begin. In the ending the foolish maidens learn the sad news that they are to be excluded. The expected event which evoked the action of parts one and two has now occurred only to find them left out. Thus again we see lines of connection binding the three

---

[32] A. M. Hunter, *Interpreting the Parables*, pp. 85–86; Jeremias, *Parables*, pp. 172–174; Michaelis, *Gleichnisse*, pp. 88–89; Smith, *Parables*, pp. 98–100.

[33] Cf. Linnemann, *Gleichnisse*, p. 130.

[34] Occasionally another character will use a descriptive adjective in pronouncing judgment (Matt. 18:32; 25:26).

parts together in a plot moving downward to distress and exclusion.

The recognition scene is not as well developed as the one in
The Talents, and we do not get as full and deep an insight into
the self-understanding of the foolish maidens as we do into
that of the one-talent man. There is a kind of preliminary
recognition when the maidens wake up and the foolish ones
realize that their oil is nearly exhausted. They recognize that
their purpose of lighting the groom's way and of participating
in the feast is threatened, but they still have the hope of success. Never do they come on their own to the conclusion that
they have been foolishly unprepared for carrying out their own
intention. They learn this to their surprise only when they are
informed by the groom that the door, now shut, is not to be
opened for them.

Again the ending is something after which there is nothing.
But that does not mean that the shutting of the door allegorically represents the eschatological exclusion from the kingdom
of God. Nor does it mean—if it does not refer to the eschatological reckoning—that the opportunity for response to God is
therefore cut off before the end.[35] The parable is not a literal
description of what is literally and finally true for all men but
is a hypothetical, imaginative work with existential implications. As such it suggests that one of the possibilities of human
existence is that existence may be lost. When a crisis is not
responsibly met, the opportunity for further action may be cut
off. When an intention is pursued with an inadequate understanding of what resources it requires, the moment of fulfill-
ment may deny the pursuer's grasp. The very fact that this
understanding is given aesthetic form, bracketed off from the

[35] Baird (Justice, pp. 129–131) holds that the coming of the bridegroom
refers to Jesus' eschatological coming, arguing that if it does not refer to the
eschaton it implies that the time for choice may be ended during history, a
conclusion which he does not wish to accept.

phenomenal world by its internal organization, strikes a note of finality. The parable's autonomy prevents our speculating about further possibilities.

The foolish maidens were as free as the wise ones to take along more oil. They simply did not. If the one-talent man in his avoidance of the risk that his role called for manifested an anxiety which saw life itself as threatening, the foolish maidens too superficially supposed that the world would take care of them, that someone else would pay the bill: if we run out of oil, our friends will help us, or the merchants will still be up, or even if we are late the groom will not lock us out. But he did.

(3) *Existential-theological interpretation.* If the one-talent man lacked that faith in a transcendent ground which would give him the freedom to risk his tangible security, the foolish maidens too presumptuously believed that their well-being was guaranteed to them no matter what they did. Even if it was a Palestinian wedding custom that anyone who had not been in the procession could not attend the feast,[36] we still are inclined by the story to identify sympathetically with the foolish maidens. Thus in view of the preparations which they had made, even if inadequate, and in view of the festive joy of the occasion, we find their abrupt exclusion shocking. This shock suggests the impingement of the divine dimension upon the everyday, the shattering effect of a crisis which breaks into our easy optimism and finds us without resources.

In The Ten Maidens time is that which transpires between an action called forth by a future expectation (the going out of the maidens to meet the bridegroom) and the occurrence of that expected event (the coming of the groom and the wedding feast). The length of this time in between is not within the control of the maidens. They cannot make the groom come any sooner than he will come; therefore, it is a time of waiting. This theme of waiting strikes a familiar note in our contem-

[36] As Oesterley claims (*Parables*, p. 135).

porary scene, for our time is often interpreted—negatively—as a time of waiting. We are waiting for Godot, and thus it is a time when "Nothing happens, nobody comes, nobody goes, it's awful."[37] Or it is a time when we are waiting for the ironical mixture of things which Ferlinghetti is waiting for:

> I am waiting for the Second Coming
> and I am waiting
> for a religious revival
> to sweep thru the state of Arizona
> and I am waiting
> for the Grapes of Wrath to be stored
> and I am waiting
> for them to prove
> that God is really American
> and I am seriously waiting
> for Billy Graham and Elvis Presley
> to exchange roles seriously
> and I am waiting
> to see God on television
> piped onto church altars
> if only they can find
> the right channel
> to tune in on
> and I am waiting
> for the Last Supper to be served again
> with a strange new appetizer
> and I am perpetually awaiting
> a rebirth of wonder.[38]

[37] Samuel Beckett, *Waiting for Godot* (New York: Grove Press, 1954, p. 27. © 1954 by Grove Press. Used by permission.

[38] Lawrence Ferlinghetti, *A Coney Island of the Mind* (New York: New Directions Books, 1958) pp. 49–50. Copyright 1955; © 1958 by Lawrence Ferlinghetti. Reprinted by permission of the publisher, New Directions Publishing Corporation, and Mr. Ferlinghetti.

What is the meaning of the ten maidens' waiting for the groom? The fact that the expected event, which gives purpose and content to the present, really does lie in the future means that the present is marked off from it as something also real. They cannot make the groom come; they can only wait for him. Therefore, the present is not a time which is to be exhausted by straining to realize the future.[39] There is time and room to live *now*. One may sleep. (We should notice that none of the maidens are condemned by the parable for sleeping.) The present, then, as time and room to live, is a gift; but it is also a demand, for uncertainty about when the expected future event will happen gives to the present a certain urgency. The maidens may sleep, but they must have sufficient oil to light the way of the groom. One may live fully in the present, but one must be attentive to the need for resources to meet a future challenge. In the case of the five maidens, as contrasted with the situation of those who were waiting for Godot, someone *did* come, in fact the very one they were expecting, but they were caught unprepared. Gift and demand are held paradoxically together. To see the present as gift alone—the folly of the five—is to be deprived by the future of any present at all.

3. *The Wedding Garment* (Matt. 22:11-14)

[11]But when the king came in to look at the guests, he saw there a man who had no wedding garment; [12]and he said to him, "Friend, how did you get in here without a wedding garment?" And he was speechless. [13]Then the king said to the attendants, "Bind him hand and foot, and cast him into the outer darkness; there men will weep and gnash their teeth." [14]For many are called, but few are chosen.

(1) *Historico-literary criticism.* The similarity of this parable

---

[39] The germ of this approach was suggested to me by Ernst Fuchs' interpretation of The Seed Growing Secretly (*Studies of the Historical Jesus*, pp. 133–134).

to rabbinic counterparts has often been pointed out,[40] but that in itself does not mean that it is not genuine, as Bultmann tends to suggest, for Jesus could well have adapted a Jewish parable to his own purposes. More serious is the fact that the vocabulary of The Wedding Garment is peculiarly Matthean.[41] However, it does not seem to be a Matthean composition as a whole. If Matthew had composed it, he would probably have made a better join between this parable and The Wedding Feast. As it is, it seems quite unfair that a man invited in without warning from the streets should be condemned for not having on the right clothes. The roughness of the connection suggests that Matthew had both The Wedding Feast and The Wedding Garment in the tradition that came to him. He put them together, lopping off the original introduction to The Wedding Garment, heavily working over its vocabulary, and adding part of 22:13 and all of 22:14. The outer darkness theme is peculiarly Matthean (cf. 8:12; 25:30), and 22:14—that only a few will be saved—fits neither The Wedding Feast nor The Wedding Garment. Since 22:11-13a is earlier than Matthew's composition, it could well be a parable of Jesus. In any case it is consistent with his teaching.

Whether the original introduction stated that some time elapsed between the invitation and the feast, giving the invited guests plenty of time to secure the proper attire (as in a rabbinic parallel), must remain questionable. But the introduction must at least have narrated the invitation and carried the assumption that the hearers would know that a wedding called for fitting clothes. The original conclusion probably said simply, "Bind him hand and foot, and throw him out."

---

[40] For example, Manson, *Sayings*, p. 226; Bultmann, *Synoptic Tradition*, p. 203.

[41] As has been shown by Gerhard Barth, "Matthew's Understanding of the Law," in *Tradition and Interpretation in Matthew*, trans. P. Scott (Philadelphia: Westminster Press, 1963), pp. 59–60, n. 9.

(2) *Literary-existential analysis.* The Wedding Garment is the shortest of the parables that are amenable to the kind of methodology that I have tried to develop. Yet it contains in concentrated and dramatic fashion the essentials of narrative art. In the beginning of the story the invitation is narrated or simply the fact that a king gave a wedding banquet. In the middle part we see an encounter between the king and one of his guests, which brings out how this guest has responded to the invitation. A proper wedding garment means, not some special festal attire, but clean clothes. This guest's failure to come in clean clothes showed disrespect for the host, the other guests, and the festal occasion.[42] The ending relates the only possible outcome of such an affront: he is to be thrown out. Thus the consequence of the invitation in part one and of the encounter in part two is drawn out in the ending. Seen in this way the parable is not an allegory about a Christian who does not live according to the law[43] but is rather an internally organized and tightly woven aesthetic object with a plot moving downward toward exclusion from a joyous society.

The very speechlessness of the guest—perhaps surprisingly—represents a keener awareness than is sometimes found in the characters of other parables. In The Ten Maidens, for example, the young women at the very end still hoped to get in and had to be told that the door was not to be opened for them. In the case of the wedding guest, however, through the encounter with the host and the latter's question to him about how he got in improperly dressed, the guest arrived at some inkling of the precariousness of his situation. His silence suggests that he had become aware of the unfittingness of his action and was able to anticipate what the only outcome could be—expulsion.

If genuine human existence is the capacity to hear a word

---

[42] Cf. Linnemann, *Gleichnisse*, p. 102; Michaelis, *Gleichnisse*, p. 161.
[43] As claimed by Smith, *Parables*, p. 206.

and to speak an appropriate answering word,[44] the wedding guest's silence speaks eloquently of his inauthenticity. When a person's understanding of existence is critically challenged, he is not able to say anything until he makes a decision about how he will now understand himself and thus restores balance and unity to his life.[45] The recognition scene of The Wedding Garment finds the guest in that moment of instability and indecision when his previous understanding of existence had been sharply questioned and its inadequacy suggested but no new understanding had been attained, with the result that he had nothing to say. And in his case—and thus possibly in anyone's case—the opportunity of making a new decision was snatched away from him.

The understanding of existence which lay behind the guest's behavior was a misunderstanding. He knew in a superficial way that a certain kind of behavior was called for; however, he did not realize that human existence *is* contextual or situational and that the character of the context requires appropriate action. If existence is situational and situations have a certain character, then to live or to attempt to live in a particular situation in an inappropriate way is to sunder oneself. The attempt of the guest to attend a wedding feast in dirty clothes manifests his split existence. The overall movement in the parable is from the guest's failure to grasp the contextual nature of existence, through the challenge to his misunderstanding, to the loss of the meaningful context in which he had hoped to exist. The guest's hopeful but uncomprehending effort ended in failure: the split in his existence is the last word about him.

(3) *Existential-theological interpretation*. The conversation between the host and the guest is evidently a private one, and

---

[44] Cf. James M. Robinson, *The New Hermeneutic*, pp. 47–48; Ebeling, "Word of God and Hermeneutic," in *New Hermeneutic*, p. 104; Fuchs, *Historical Jesus*, pp. 89, 211.

[45] Cf. Fuchs, *Historical Jesus*, pp. 221–222.

the host might have quietly eased our dirty man out of the hall.
The fact that the host rather called his servants and dramatically ordered them to bind the guest hand and foot and throw
him out surprises us somewhat and again suggests the divine
action upon human existence.

God's hand is present to preside over the dissolution which
occurs when the God-given structure of existence is violated.
Man is limited in that he cannot choose certain courses and
stances and also avoid disastrous consequences. The man of
Christian faith lives as one who is becoming, in between the
radical offer of forgiveness and the demand for radical
obedience—the essence of Jesus' message.[46] One must live appropriately to the situation of grace. This is to have a unified
self. The invitation of the king to the wedding feast was a gift
which internally entailed the demand for clean clothes. The
neglect of the demand resulted in losing the gift. The attempt
to live within the gift of God while rejecting the inseparable
demand to respond appropriately to grace is a misguided effort
which splits one's existence and issues in the loss of the situation where grace is present.

4. The Wicked Tenants (Mark 12:1-9)

¹And he began to speak to them in parables. "A man planted
a vineyard, and set a hedge around it, and dug a pit for the wine
press, and built a tower, and let it out to tenants, and went into
another country. ²When the time came, he sent a servant to the
tenants, to get from them some of the fruit of the vineyard. ³And
they took him and beat him, and sent him away emptyhanded.
⁴Again he sent to them another servant, and they wounded him in
the head, and treated him shamefully. ⁵And he sent another, and
him they killed; and so with many others, some they beat and some
they killed. ⁶He had still one other, a beloved son; finally he sent
him to them, saying, 'They will respect my son.' ⁷But those ten-

---

[46] Cf. Herbert Braun, "Der Sinn der neutestamentlichen Christologie,"
Zeitschrift für Theologie und Kirche, 54 (1957), 346, 347, 350.

ants said to one another, 'This is the heir; come, let us kill him, and the inheritance will be ours.' [8]And they took him and killed him, and cast him out of the vineyard. [9]What will the owner of the vineyard do? He will come and destroy the tenants, and give the vineyard to others."

(1) *Historico-literary criticism.* In the thinking of some, the question of this parable's genuineness is tied up with whether it is an allegory. The content is held to be artificial, and it is said that it can be read intelligibly only as an allegory. The allegorical content, it is claimed, came from the church; therefore the parable in its present form could not be a word of Jesus.[47] On the other hand, it is possible to take it as originally an allegory and also a genuine word of Jesus.[48] And it is true that its being an allegory would not in itself rule out the parable's genuineness, but we must decide whether it is an allegory or not in order to interpret it properly.

It seems to have been demonstrated that the relationship depicted between the owner and his tenants is realistic, and not artificial.[49] However, allegorical features remain, especially in the Markan version. The details of Mark 12:1 make a clear reference to the vineyard song of Isa. 5, and the generalizing summary statement of 12:5b refers to Israel's increasing rebelliousness. The reference to the killing of the servants in 12:5 also anticipates the murder of the son. The use of the adjective *agapētos* of the son appears to be a Markan christological motif which connects the parable with the baptism and transfiguration of Jesus (cf. Mark 1:11; 9:7) in which stories Jesus is portrayed as the beloved Son. In Luke (20:9) and the Gospel of

---

[47] Cf. Bultmann, *Synoptic Tradition*, pp. 177, 205; R. M. Grant, *The Letter and the Spirit*, p. 44.

[48] Cf. Matthew Black, "The Parables as Allegory," pp. 280–283.

[49] We may be on more certain ground to say that the owner, for a reason not given, was unable to return to his lands (Michaelis, *Gleichnisse*, p. 117) rather than to conjecture that he was a foreign, absentee landlord (Dodd, *Parables*, pp. 96–97; Jeremias, *Parables*, pp. 74–75).

Thomas (65 [66]) the reference to Isa. 5 is much more allusive than in Mark and therefore deflects the attention less from the parable to the source of the vineyard image. Luke and Thomas also omit the generalizing summary in Mark 12:5b as well as the murder of the servants. In Thomas, moreover, *agapētos* is lacking. In my judgment the parable is a genuine saying of Jesus, but the original version lacked the detailed reference to Isa. 5, the summary given in Mark 12:5b, the murder of the third servant, and the use of *agapētos*. Whether there were three servants beaten (Luke), or only two (Thomas), is impossible to say. The Lukan version has the rule of three plus one, thus emphasizing the son. Thomas' rendition brings the son within the rule of three.

A comparison of this parable with Jesus' other narrative parables is what suggests that the least allegorical version is the most original. Even so, just the allusive reference to the vineyard and the beating of the servants must have referred subsidiarily to Israel and her rejection of God's messengers. And the "son" possibly refers to the climactic coming of Jesus but without specific christological implications. Thus this parable is more nearly allegorical than (most of) Jesus' other narrative parables, but the pattern of connections is still primarily within the story and runs only subsidiarily to the outside. If, then, the wicked tenants refer to the Jewish leaders of Jesus' day as well as to Israel or its leaders through the centuries, what understanding of existence is being attributed to them?

(2) *Literary-existential analysis.* It is claimed by Baird[50] that the figure of the owner dominates the story, while Michaelis[51] seems to be most interested in the question of his son. From the standpoint of the story itself both of these approaches are somewhat eccentric in view of the fact that the formal shape of the story derives from the experience of the wicked tenants.

[50] *Justice*, p. 67.
[51] *Gleichnisse*, pp. 121–122.

The beginning relates that a man let out his vineyard to tenants and went away. In the middle part we see what happened when he attempted to collect the proceeds which were rightfully due to him, and we have the hint of an insight into why the tenants behaved as they did. The ending tells about—or at least suggests—the destruction which will come to the tenants as a result of their behavior. Again beginning, middle, and end are interlocked within a downward moving plot.

It is impossible to say whether Jesus' question—"What will the owner of the vineyard do?"—was originally answered by Jesus himself (Mark 12:9)[52] or by the Jewish rulers (Matt. 21:23, 41).[53] Perhaps the best suggestion is that the parable originally ended simply with Jesus' question, which implied the destruction of the tenants.[54] But both the logic of the story and its connection with Isa. 5 require some hint of judgment. It is true that the Gospel of Thomas has neither the question nor the answer, but Thomas' addition of "He who has ears, let him hear" shows that he has tampered with the ending. The fact that the conclusion of the parable takes the form—wholly or partially—of a question to the audience gives the parable somewhat less aesthetic autonomy and distance than is usually the case with Jesus' narrative parables.

In the middle part of the story we see that the tenants were calculating how they might seize what was not theirs even if they had to commit murder in order to do so. Their violence was so wanton that they need not have had any particular religious presuppositions to realize that what they were doing violated basic human norms for living in the world with other men. Thus they must have recognized that their actions were wrong even though they did not recognize until it was too late —if they recognized at all—that they would bring about their

[52] Oesterley, *Parables*, pp. 119–120.
[53] Dodd, *Parables*, pp. 98–99.
[54] Smith, *Parables*, p. 224.

own destruction. They hoped for the success of their violent plot. If there was actually little chance of their being successful, that points, not to the unreality of the story, but to the blind folly that infuses human evil.

The image of man which we see in this parable is that of a being who tries to possess as much as he possibly can regardless of the cost to others and as a result brings about his own destruction. If *Macbeth* is the supreme tragedy of a figure who gives free reign "to the mutiny at the heart of man,"[55] The Wicked Tenants is a miniature tragedy on the same theme. We are also reminded of Kurtz in Joseph Conrad's *Heart of Darkness* who is described as one who "wanted to swallow all the air, all the earth, all the men before him."[56] There is, moreover, in *Heart of Darkness* a pattern of connections which helps us to grasp the understanding and state of existence which lie behind and are implied in the action of the wicked tenants. Kurtz is represented as a hollow man to whom the wilderness had whispered "irresistibly fascinating" things about himself. As a result he came to belong to the powers of darkness and to believe that "everything belonged to him." He was a man who "knew no restraint."[57]

The tenants' intention to kill and to possess must rest on a similar existential flaw, and we are reminded of the saying attributed to Jesus about the man who, having been relieved of one demon, soon had his emptiness filled by seven others (Matt. 12:43-45). This suggests that human evil has both its negative and its positive sides. There may be at the heart of man an emptiness, an abyss, which becomes the base of operations for powers that prompt man to unrestrained violence against his fellows. One who acts out such an existence is

[55] Philip Wheelwright, *The Burning Fountain*, p. 208.
[56] *Joseph Conrad's Heart of Darkness*, ed. L. F. Dean (Englewood Cliffs, N. J.: Prentice-Hall, 1961), p. 50.
[57] *Ibid.*, pp. 40–41, 48, 56.

already dead within and inevitably brings about his physical destruction as well. While in this and in Jesus' other parables human evil and its judgment pertain primarily to human relationships, the use of the vineyard image here and the theme of expulsion from the vineyard may suggest that injustice and violence not only shatter human relationships but disturb man's relationship with nature also. Especially does the presence of Isa. 5 in the background suggest the enmity with nature which results from human ruptures (Isa. 5:5–7).

(3) *Existential-theological interpretation.* When The Wicked Tenants is seen as a parable of unfaith, then sin becomes man's self-centered effort to reject any and all limitations which the being and will of God impose upon him. Man's self-defensive drive for security, engendered by a lack of faith in the benevolence of the universe, may express itself in more than one way. If man cannot believe that there is a transcendent reality which undergirds him and fills his emptiness, he may act as little as possible or he may be driven to violent action. In both cases the power that would have sustained him had he been responsible causes his downfall when he is irresponsible.

5. *The Unforgiving Servant* (Matt. 18:23-35)

[23]Therefore the kingdom of heaven may be compared to a king who wished to settle accounts with his servants. [24]When he began the reckoning, one was brought to him who owed him ten thousand talents; [25]and as he could not pay, his lord ordered him to be sold, with his wife and children and all that he had, and payment to be made. [26]So the servant fell on his knees, imploring him, "Lord, have patience with me, and I will pay you everything." [27]And out of pity for him the lord of that servant released him and forgave him the debt. [28]But that same servant, as he went out, came upon one of his fellow servants who owed him a hundred denarii; and seizing him by the throat he said, "Pay what you owe." [29]So his fellow servant fell down and besought him, "Have patience with me, and I will pay you." [30]He refused and went and

put him in prison till he should pay the debt. [31]When his fellow servants saw what had taken place, they were greatly distressed, and they went and reported to their lord all that had taken place. [32]Then his lord summoned him and said to him, "You wicked servant! I forgave you all that debt because you besought me; [33]and should not you have had mercy on your fellow servant, as I had mercy on you?" [34]And in anger his lord delivered him to the jailers, till he should pay all his debt. [35]So also my heavenly Father will do to every one of you, if you do not forgive your brother from your heart.

(1) *Historico-literary criticism.* According to Linnemann[58] the fact that there is nothing in the parable (18:23-34) about repeated forgiveness means that its connection with Matt. 18: 21–22 is not original. Both Matt. 18:21–22 and the parable do, however, deal with forgiveness; and Oesterley[59] has pointed out that making loose connections is typical of Jewish parabolic practice and is, therefore, no argument against the originality of the connection. Since Matt. 18 as a whole, however, is composed of materials from various sources, one is inclined to think that the connection between 18:21–22 and the parable was first made by Matthew.

The colossal size of the debt suggests that the parable is speaking about a king and one of his satraps.[60] The compulsory selling of a man and his family to pay a debt also points to the gentile coloring of the fictional elements,[61] though this should

[58] *Gleichnisse,* p. 111.

[59] *Parables,* pp. 93–94.

[60] Jeremias, *Parables,* p. 210. Michaelis (*Gleichnisse,* p. 191) suggests that since the king is referred to as *kyrios* (18:25, 27, 31, 32, 34), except in 18:23, Matthew may have substituted *basileus* for an original *kyrios* in order to emphasize the parable's connection with the kingdom of heaven. Whatever the original wording, the large sum of money probably suggests a royal situation.

[61] Cf. Jeremias, *Parables,* p. 211; Günther Bornkamm, *Jesus of Nazareth,* p. 86. Of the passages which Oesterley (*Parables,* p. 95) cites to prove that the parable envisions a Jewish setting (Exod. 22:3; Lev. 25:39; II Kings 4:1; Neh. 5:5) only II Kings 4:1 is even possibly pertinent, and Jeremias cites rabbinic sources which forbid the sale of a wife.

not be taken to mean that the parable originated in gentile territory and is not a parable of Jesus.

Matt. 18:35 appears to be Matthew's conclusion to the whole of chapter 18 rather than the original application of the parable, and it reflects Matthew's legalistic tendency.

(2) *Literary-existential analysis.* It has been held that it is the king who gives meaning and coherence to the parable,[62] and the king does obviously have an important role, but from the standpoint of the parable itself, it is the unforgiving servant's story; that is, his changing fate determines the narrative form. To ignore this turns the parable into an illustrated exhortation and forfeits its aesthetic power. The four parables that we have considered thus far manifest a more or less steady downward movement in their plots. The protagonist begins in a good situation and moves to catastrophe. In The Unforgiving Servant, on the other hand, we have the somewhat more complex double movement from a bad to a good to a bad, or worse, situation. A potentially and hopefully comic movement is overcome by tragedy.

In the first part of the parable the servant is found in a threatening crisis. Since he could not pay the huge debt which he owed, his lord intended to sell him and his wife and children into slavery. In view of the fact that the sale of his family would not even begin to pay the debt,[63] we see that the king's threat is an expression of his anger.[64] The servant asked for time to make payment—though the situation was hopeless— and must have been greatly surprised when the lord responded to his plea by cancelling the debt completely.

In the middle part we see what effect this surprising and unearned improvement in his situation had on him. That it

[62] Baird, *Justice*, p. 64.

[63] The price of a slave was five hundred to two thousand denarii, and there were ten thousand denarii in one talent. Cf. Linnemann, *Gleichnisse*, p. 114. The servant owed ten thousand talents.

[64] Cf. Jeremias, *Parables*, p. 211.

had no effect is made shockingly offensive by the fact that he met his fellow servant immediately upon leaving the king, when he should have been especially aware that he had been the recipient of mercy, and by the casting of the fellow servant's plea for time in the same words which he himself had used. The first servant owed a tremendous debt which he could never have paid, and mercy was extended to him. He was owed a small debt which could have been paid had he allowed a little time, but he exacted harsh justice.[65] The king, on being informed of his servant's behavior, reminded him that he should have responded to mercy with mercy (18:33).

In the ending (18:34) the king in anger delivered his servant to the torturers—or jailers. In the beginning we have a dramatic encounter, in the middle, the response to the encounter, and in the conclusion, the consequence of the response: an interlocking plot moving finally downward to catastrophe.

Linnemann maintains that the real interest of the parable, the point of comparison, is 18:33. She holds this on the ground that if 18:34 were the point, the speech of the king in 18:33 would not have been needed, for the speech is without significance for the issue of the action and expects no answer from the servant. Linnemann goes on to say that the fact that the emphasis is usually at the end is no argument against her position because 18:34 is the necessary completion of 18:33. Matt. 18:33 was spoken as a window for the hearers of the parable.[66]

In response to Linnemann it should be said that neither 18:33 nor 18:34 is *the* point. If we want to use the term "point," it should be used to refer to the meaning of the total, organically unified structure of form-and-content. If critical interpretation can, by the use of propositional language, express that total meaning in one sentence, that is no substitute

[65] Cf. Linnemann, *Gleichnisse*, pp. 19, 115.
[66] *Ibid.*, p. 116.

for the parable itself. Yet it should be said that 18:33 does come close to summing up the thematic side of the parable.

Matt. 18:33 is not just a window to the hearers but also a mirror which reflects on the relationship of the unforgiving servant to the king and to his fellow servant and which relates itself to the tragic denouement in 18:34. Actually the aesthetic force of the parable overcomes Linnemann's one-point approach and enables her to see that 18:34 is necessary for 18:33. How then can it be denied that 18:33 is necessary for 18:34? Each of the verses is necessary for the other, and 18:33 is also the needed link between 18:32 and 18:34. To receive (18:32) without giving (18:33) is self-destructive (18:34). Just as 18:34 gives the consequences of a certain kind of attitude, so 18:33 is needed to clarify why catastrophe occurred. Thus 18:33 is fused into the narrative so that the fact that it expects no answer does not mean that it is only a window to the audience.

In the opening crisis it had not occurred to the servant that the debt might be cancelled. He thought in terms of claims made and claims paid, and pleaded for time to make his payment. He must have known that he could not really have followed through, but in his extremity he was grasping for straws. Because he at least did not place the blame for his plight on someone else, we are prepared to be sympathetic with him. Our sympathy recoils, however, when we witness his behavior in part two. His understanding of human relationships—that they are constituted by claims justly made and necessarily paid —had been challenged but not altered by the mercy shown him. At the end he still had not come to recognize what mercy does and had to be told—after it was too late—what he should have grasped on his own and what the consequence of his failure would be.

That he was to be delivered to the torturers until he should pay his debt meant that he would never escape them, for his debt was unimaginably great.

141

The parable suggests that one may unexpectedly find an openness or receptivity in others which delivers one from a pressing problem and opens up a surprising new possibility for existence. If the new situation is not internalized, however, so that one becomes open to others and can relinquish claims, then the new situation is lost. To accept what is undeserved from others without extending such graciousness dries up the capacity to receive, and one's isolation is thus made complete. The final physical isolation of the unforgiving servant from his lord and from his fellow servants only confirms the estrangement from others which was implicit in his self-understanding from the beginning and which was never shattered.

The Greek word *(dei)* behind the "should" in the king's "Should you not have had mercy?" (18:33) is characteristically used of the divine necessity (cf. Mark 8:31; 13:7; Matt. 23:23; Luke 22:7; 24:26; John 3:14).[67] The strength of this word suggests the inescapability of the existential reality implied in the parable.

(3) *Existential-theological interpretation.* The element of the measureless and the surprising which pervades the parable[68] suggests the impingement of the divine and the finality of the issues involved. The immensity of the servant's debt, for example—ten thousand talents—becomes more vivid for us when we recognize that the annual revenue of Herod the Great was not more than nine hundred talents.[69]

To see the parable as expressing an existential movement (as discussed above) obviates the tendency to a legalistic interpretation of the parable which is often found: God forgives

[67] *Ibid.*
[68] Cf. Bornkamm, *Jesus*, p. 86.
[69] Cf. Linnemann, *Gleichnisse*, p. 114. The annual imperial taxes of all Judea, Idumea, and Samaria were only six hundred talents, and Galilee and Perea added only two hundred more to this (cf. Oesterley, *Parables*, p. 95; Baird, *Justice*, p. 64; Linnemann, *Gleichnisse*, p. 114).

us as we forgive our fellows.[70] On the contrary, it is not that our forgiveness of others wins God's forgiveness for us but rather that his forgiveness confers upon us the capacity to forgive. The one who has really experienced forgiveness *will* forgive. Thus the emphasis is on a total situation which inclines one to be forgiving rather than on the *demand* to forgive, though the latter is not wholly absent.[71] Forgiveness is not an isolated occurrence but an order of existence.[72] To have our legalistic understanding of life shattered by the transcendent as that which accepts and sustains us despite our offensiveness is to be opened to others in their offensiveness. To have the structure of our existence opened by and to the transcendent and to have it opened to others are two sides of the same existential reality, and one side cannot be present without the other. To approach this from the other side, one who takes the risk of being open and vulnerable to others does so because he is sustained by the transcendent, whether or not he knows it (cf. Matt. 25:31-46). The man who rejects the order of openness, forgiveness, and vulnerability places himself in the order of claims which will isolate and crush him. This was the tragedy of the unforgiving servant.

Although this parable does not have a legalistic meaning, it does obviously suggest that a certain understanding and way of existence are self-destructive. This, however, is not really in contradiction—as Fuchs[73] claims—with Matt. 5:45, which states that the sun and rain come for the unjust as well as for the just. The two passages refer to two different levels of reality. Matt. 5:45 presents man over against the "givenness" of

[70] Cf. Jeremias, *Parables*, pp. 213, 214; Hunter, *Parables*, p. 71; Manson, *Sayings*, p. 213.
[71] Cf. Bultmann, *Jesus and the Word*, pp. 183, 211.
[72] Cf. Linnemann, *Gleichnisse*, pp. 117–119.
[73] *Historical Jesus*, p. 153.

nature, and here man's actions have no effect. But the parable presents a man in relation to the structure of human existence, and here man's abuses can bring about his destruction.

In concluding this chapter it might be noted that in The Unforgiving Servant tragedy results basically from the failure to respond appropriately to grace while in the other four parables the emphasis is on the failure to meet a demand responsibly, though the note of grace is not wholly lacking in the others nor the note of demand in this one.

5

The Comic Parables

It should be recalled that the category of comedy is being used in the broad sense of a plot that moves upward toward the well-being of the protagonist and his inclusion in a desirable society. Here the comic view will be briefly but somewhat more fully developed than it has been thus far and something of the distinctiveness of Jesus' comic parables will be indicated.

According to Nathan Scott, tragic and comic man are distinguished in that tragic man is burdened and embarrassed by his finitude while comic man is the image of human actuality. Comic man is not imprisoned by nor resentful about being human, and comedy presents the whole truth that men have bodies and need food and sleep as well as have aspirations which might shake the cosmos.[1] Although this distinction is probably valid in general, it does not apply to the difference between Jesus' tragic and comic parables. The reason is that *both* classes of Jesus' parables are in the low mimetic mode and employ the imagery of everyday realism; therefore, both classes portray man in his human actuality. Moreover, the element of the surprising which fractures the realism "eschatologically" is as characteristic of the comic parables as of the tragic ones.

As Scott has pointed out, there are two types of comic

[1] Nathan A. Scott, Jr., "The Bias of Comedy and the Narrow Escape into Faith," pp. 19–21.

145

protagonist. The first becomes the object of our unsympathetic laughter because of his deviation from a legitimate human norm. The second type has heroic proportions, and if he is eccentric, it is because he is so deeply rooted in the human stuff. No matter how many scrapes he has, his energies remain unimpaired, and the central moment in a comedy with such a protagonist is the reassertion of humanness.[2]

In the light of this second motif we may say with Christopher Fry that comedy is not simply an escape from truth into mirth but rather an escape from despair into faith. It manifests the intuition to trust the situation that we were born into.[3] The comic protagonist thus conceived must have a stature fit for tragedy. He must be able to affirm life, take death upon himself, and move toward joy. It is interesting that Fry sees the Book of Job as the great reservoir of comedy[4] when Job has so often been seen as tragedy.[5] Certainly in The Prodigal Son, Jesus' classic comic story, death is assimilated and overcome, and the note of joy is finally sounded. Northrop Frye's comment is quite appropriate that it is altogether characteristic of anything explicitly Christian that the tragic should be a prelude to comedy.[6]

In Jesus' comic parables it is not that a man has within himself the resources for the reassertion of his whole humanity but rather that there comes to him from beyond himself a new possibility that was not at his disposal. When these parables are seen as defining the divine-human relationship, then it is the grace of God which enables the passage from death to life.

[2] Ibid., pp. 28–32.
[3] Christopher Fry, "Comedy," in The New Orpheus, ed. Nathan A. Scott, Jr. (New York: Sheed and Ward, 1964), pp. 286–287.
[4] Ibid., p. 288.
[5] Cf., for example, Richard B. Sewall, The Vision of Tragedy, pp. 9, 19, 21.
[6] Northrop Frye, Anatomy of Criticism, p. 215.

146

It has been denied that literature of the extreme situation can present a Christian resolution of man's plight that is aesthetically convincing: the theology of the author will inevitably intrude.[7] To this it should be said that conversion has been one of the major motifs of twentieth-century literature,[8] and it is no more impossible in principle to render a Christian conversion aesthetically satisfying (though it has seldom been done) than any other kind of conversion, unless the critic rigidly applies some kind of positivistic norm. The prodigal son is pictured in an extreme situation, and he is delivered. Admittedly the strategies of a biblical parable and of a novel presenting a Christian conversion are not exactly the same. They are not so different, however, that the parable may not be suggestive of how it might be done in a novel.

1. The Workers in the Vineyard (Matt. 20:1-16)

[1]For the kingdom of heaven is like a householder who went out early in the morning to hire laborers for his vineyard. [2]After agreeing with the laborers for a denarius a day, he sent them into his vineyard. [3]And going out about the third hour he saw others standing idle in the market place; [4]and to them he said, "You go into the vineyard too, and whatever is right I will give you." So they went. [5]Going out again about the sixth hour and the ninth hour, he did the same. [6]And about the eleventh hour he went out and found others standing; and he said to them, "Why do you stand here idle all day?" [7]They said to him, "Because no one has hired us." He said to them, "You go into the vineyard too." [8] And when evening came, the owner of the vineyard said to his steward, "Call the laborers and pay them their wages, beginning with the last, up to the first." [9]And when those hired about the eleventh hour came, each of them received a denarius. [10]Now when the first came, they thought they would receive more; but each of them also received a denarius. [11]And on receiving it they grumbled at

[7] Murray Krieger, *The Tragic Vision*, pp. 263–266.
[8] Cf. R. W. B. Lewis, *The Picaresque Saint* (Philadelphia and New York: J. B. Lippincott, Keystone Books, 1961), pp. 27–28.

the householder, [12]saying, "These last worked only one hour, and you have made them equal to us who have borne the burden of the day and the scorching heat." [13]But he replied to one of them, "Friend, I am doing you no wrong; did you not agree with me for a denarius? [14]Take what belongs to you, and go; I choose to give to this last as I give to you. [15]Am I not allowed to do what I choose with what belongs to me? Or do you begrudge my generosity?" [16]So the last will be first, and the first last.

(1) *Historico-literary criticism.* This parable (Matt. 20:1-15) was placed by Matthew in its present (Markan) context as an illustration of the thought that the first will be last and the last, first (Matt. 19:30; Mark 10:31). Matt. 19:30 was then repeated, with slightly altered wording, in 20:16 as the conclusion to the parable in order to emphasize the connection which Matthew wanted to make between 19:30 and the parable. That the connection between the parable and Matt. 19:30 is not original, however, is seen from the fact that the verse appears in Mark without the parable (10:31) and in Luke both without the parable and in an entirely different context (13:30).

The idea of reversal of rank—the first last, and the last first —does not really get at the meaning of the parable.[9] The connection was made by Matthew simply because the householder told his steward to pay first those who were hired last (20:8b). This latter point is not simply an unimportant detail[10] from the standpoint of the parable as a story, however. The payment of those hired last had to take place in the presence of those who were hired first and who had worked all day in order that the full-day workers might see how much the late comers were paid. This was necessary in order to elicit the dissatisfaction of those hired first and to set up, thereby, the dramatic

---

[9] Cf. Joachim Jeremias, *The Parables of Jesus*, pp. 35–36; Wilhelm Michaelis, *Die Gleichnisse Jesu*, p. 180.
[10] As claimed by Jeremias, *Parables*, p. 35.

conflict between these dissatisfied workers and the house-holder.[11]

It is the present context of the parable in Matthew that directs it to Jesus' disciples.[12] It was probably originally told with reference to Jesus' opponents in order to defend his association with the sinners and to attack any legalistic merit doctrine.[13]

The vineyard image again allusively associates the parable with Israel's story (cf. Isa. 5).

(2) *Literary-existential analysis.* While, as we shall see, The Workers in the Vineyard manifests a stronger allegorical tendency than most of Jesus' other narrative parables, its aesthetic form does resist the kind of allegorizing which sees the hiring of the workers as the action of the kingdom of God in history, the wage settlement as the final judgment, and the denarius as eternal life.[14] Such an interpretation superimposes a preconceived pattern upon the parable, prevents its being a new word, and vitiates its attention grasping aesthetic function.

There is a real sense, however, in which this parable is the householder's story,[15] and this fact gives it its allegorical tendency. The householder probably has a relatively more prominent role throughout the story than the "master" figure in any of the other narrative parables, and this emphasis is augmented —in view of the law of end stress[16]—by the fact that the entire

---

[11] Cf. Ernst Fuchs, *Studies of the Historical Jesus,* p. 154; Eta Linnemann, *Die Gleichnisse Jesu,* pp. 89–90; Michaelis, *Gleichnisse,* p. 175; B. T. D. Smith, *The Parables of the Synoptic Gospels,* p. 185.

[12] Cf. Jeremias, *Parables,* pp. 37–38; Linnemann, *Gleichnisse,* p. 50. Michaelis (*Gleichnisse,* p. 180) argues that it was originally a disciple parable.

[13] Cf. Jeremias, *Parables,* pp. 37–38.

[14] As in J. Arthur Baird, *The Justice of God in the Teaching of Jesus,* pp. 209–211.

[15] Thus Jeremias, *Parables,* p. 136; Fuchs, "Bemerkungen zur Gleichnisauslegung," p. 347; *Historical Jesus,* p. 33; Michaelis, *Gleichnisse,* pp. 177–178.

[16] Cf. Smith, *Parables,* p. 36.

conclusion (20:13-15) is made up of a rather detailed statement of the householder's position. We have the phenomenon that he has a very prominent place and yet he does not give the parable its formal shape. He is not drawn into the vicissitudes of the plot. Therefore, he tends to point allegorically out of the story. But the householder image probably points more directly to Jesus, as the material part of the parable and especially to his meals with and his conduct toward sinners, than it does to God.[17]

There is, on the other hand, another sense in which this parable is the story of the grumbling, full-day workers; and exegesis has usually not been sufficiently attentive to this fact. These workers are allowed a recognition scene, and it is their changing fortune which gives the parable its formal shape. Thus in tension with the allegorical tendency is an internal, aesthetic unity.

The beginning tells about a householder who hired workers for his vineyard at various times during the day, hiring some just for the last working hour. Whether or not the parable presupposes that the rainy season was about to set in,[18] the householder's repeated trips to the market place to hire workers suggest some kind of urgency. The last workers hired, who worked only an hour, may or may not have been sincere in their claim that they were idle because they could not get work. In any case, the parable does not base their being hired or the payment of a full day's wage on their undeserved misfortune.[19] At the time of hiring nothing is said about the amount that would be paid to the workers who were employed for one hour since that would have spoiled the dramatic effect of the surprising payment in the next part.[20]

[17] Cf. Fuchs, "Bemerkungen," pp. 347–348; *Historical Jesus*, pp. 34–36.
[18] As Jeremias (*Parables*, p. 136) claims.
[19] Cf. Linnemann, *Gleichnisse*, p. 88.
[20] Cf. *ibid.*, p. 89.

In the middle part we see the settling up with the workers at the day's end and the complaint of the full-day workers that they had been treated unfairly. In the ending the householder defended and interpreted his action and dismissed the complaining workers from his presence. Thus we have an interlocking plot moving downward from the well-being of the full-day workers to their exclusion from the presence of a good man.

The plot movement means that The Workers in the Vineyard could have been discussed with the tragic parables and in a sense should have been, but there are also reasons for including it among the comic ones:

(a) The exclusion of the grumbling workers from a desirable society is not as emphatic as in The Talents, The Ten Maidens, The Wedding Garment, and The Unforgiving Servant.

(b) In four of the tragic parables catastrophe occurs, as we have seen, primarily because of the failure to fulfill a demand. In The Workers in the Vineyard, on the other hand, the emphasis is on the fact that tragedy is estrangement from a gracious benefactor, and the quality of that graciousness is stressed. The downfall results from rejecting a comic-redemptive possibility. This is also true in The Unforgiving Servant, but there the exclusion from well-being is much more striking than in The Workers in the Vineyard. The Unforgiving Servant emphasizes the fall of one who refuses to live in the order of mercy, while the present parable emphasizes the graciousness that is rejected.

(c) There are comic characters in the parable—the workers hired at the end of the day who benefited from the surprising generosity of the householder. There are also characters in The Talents and The Ten Maidens who move to well-being, but they are not as prominent as the comic characters in The Workers in the Vineyard. In the latter parable the central conflict revolves around the treatment of the comic characters, but in The Talents and The Ten Maidens the conflict is strictly be-

151

tween the master figure and the tragic characters. The cross-currents of the tragic and comic in The Workers in the Vineyard might be explained partially by saying that the tragic characters—the grumbling full-day workers—are the "blocking characters" (characters who seek to impede the comic movement) of a potentially ironic comedy, but their role has been enlarged to the point that what might have been an ironic comedy has been tipped over into an ironic tragedy. The subsequent discussion will show that their fate was certainly ironic.

In summarizing the discussion up to this juncture it might be said that from the plot standpoint The Workers in the Vineyard is a tragedy, but from the thematic standpoint it is a comedy. Moreover, the theme of the householder's generosity gives the parable its allegorical tendency which stands in a certain tension with the internal connections.

The flaw in the grumbling workers which comes to expression in the recognition scene (20:12) is more serious than an envy which cannot tolerate kindness shown to others.[21] If there was envy, it was only symptomatic of their feeling a threat to their deep-seated understanding of existence. The fact that they insisted on the application of a merit system—reward should be exactly proportionate to achievement—shows that they believed themselves capable of maintaining their position in the world, of deserving their reward. If someone, however, is rewarded, not on the basis of his own achievement, but on the basis of another's generosity, then there is an incalculable element in human relationships, and the sense of being able to provide one's own security is seriously challenged. In the face of this challenge the grumbling workers still insisted on a merit order. Their desire to have their security within their own grasp caused them to see the incalculable, not as graciousness, but as injustice. Rather than seeing themselves as self-centered they accused the householder of unfairness.

[21] As Michaelis (*Gleichnisse*, pp. 175–178) suggests.

In all of the other narrative parables—tragic and comic—the crisis and conflict of the protagonist result from some flaw in his action, some violation by him of the normative order. He is in some sense called to account by a superior figure (or by himself). In The Workers in the Vineyard, on the other hand, there is no flaw in the complaining workers' action, that is, in their work, for which they are called to account. Rather they initiated the conflict as a result of their interpretation of their actions in relation to other realities, and in so doing revealed their flawed self-understanding. In the recognition scene itself their external situation was not threatened. It was only their self-understanding which was questioned by the surprising thing which they had witnessed. But because they did not recognize the true nature of the incalculable and insisted on strict justice where graciousness was actually to be found, in the end they were estranged from the source of graciousness. In pursuing what they regarded as their interests they annulled their best possibilities. The irony of their action is brought out by playing up the goodness from which they estranged themselves. This estrangement confirmed what had been true for them all along.

The tragic conclusion of the complaining workers' story is the householder's command: "Take what is yours and go." The organic union of this command with the whole parable and the indispensability of taking it into consideration in interpreting the parable are often, if not usually, ignored. The result of ignoring this matter is a tendency in theological interpretation to say that the parable does not teach that reward is wholly by grace. It is suggested by some scholars that according to the parable God deals with some people on the basis of merit (the full-day workers) and with others according to grace (the one-hour workers).[22] The effort is then made by

[22] Cf. Jeremias, *Parables*, p. 36; T. W. Manson, *The Sayings of Jesus*, p. 218.

153

these interpreters to avoid this unwelcome conclusion by falling back on the one-point approach to the parables. It is said that the real point of the parable is not to make a distinction between grace and merit but rather to emphasize how much the one-hour workers received[23] or to affirm that there are no distinctions in the kingdom.[24]

A more appropriate approach would be to take into account the expulsion of the grumbling workers. It is true that they would have gone home anyway, but the fact that the parable explicitly relates the householder's order to them to go makes their going a dismissal. When this is seen in connection with their complaint about the householder's generosity to the one-hour workers, then the parable does not teach that God deals with some on the basis of merit. That is, it does not teach that while some need grace, others do not, but rather suggests why some do not receive it. Because of their impenetrable legalistic understanding of existence, grounded in the effort to effect their own security, they exclude themselves from the source of grace.

(3) *Existential-theological interpretation.* The householder's frequent trips to the market place exhibit throughout improbable, though not impossible, behavior. His striking action reaches a climax when he pays the last workers a full day's wage for one hour's work.[25] This surprising element woven into a realistic story suggests to us again that the divine dimension may cross our everyday reality to produce a crisis of ultimate importance in the midst of the ordinary. Our very existence depends on whether we will accept God's gracious dealings, his dealings which shatter our calculations about how things ought to be ordered in the world.

The householder's last statement—that he can do as he

[23] Jeremias, *Parables,* p. 36.
[24] Manson, *Sayings,* p. 219.
[25] Cf. Fuchs, *Historical Jesus,* p. 33; Linnemann, *Gleichnisse,* pp. 88–89.

chooses with what is his—taken by itself might suggest that God is merely arbitrary. But in the context of the parable it means that he is gracious. God gives to the man who has nothing a place to exist meaningfully before himself, and he does this as an expression of his own generosity and without regard for human considerations of merit. Man, however, may be too calculating to accept the risks in such dealings. We see that the formal tension—between the relatively strong allegorical pointing to the graciousness of God and the internally organized tragic plot—embodies the existential tension that while the ultimate meaning of life is God's gracious dealing, man may yet bring about the tragic loss of his existence.

2. *The Unjust Steward* (Luke 16:1-9)

[1]He also said to the disciples, "There was a rich man who had a steward, and charges were brought to him that this man was wasting his goods. [2]And he called him and said to him, 'What is this that I hear about you? Turn in the account of your stewardship, for you can no longer be steward.' [3]And the steward said to himself, 'What shall I do, since my master is taking the stewardship away from me? I am not strong enough to dig, and I am ashamed to beg. [4]I have decided what to do, so that people may receive me into their houses when I am put out of the stewardship.' [5]So, summoning his master's debtors one by one, he said to the first, 'How much do you owe my master?' [6]He said, 'A hundred measures of oil.' And he said to him, 'Take your bill, and sit down quickly and write fifty.' [7]Then he said to another, 'And how much do you owe?' He said, 'A hundred measures of wheat.' He said to him, 'Take your bill, and write eighty.' [8]The master commended the dishonest steward for his prudence; for the sons of this world are wiser in their own generation than the sons of light. [9]And I tell you, make friends for yourselves by means of unrighteous mammon, so that when it fails they may receive you into the eternal habitations."

(1) *Historico-literary criticism.* Our main problem here is determining where the parable originally ended. It seems clear

155

that 16:9, 16:10-12, and 16:13 were originally connected neither with the parable nor with each other[26] and were perhaps first linked together by Luke on the basis of the catchword "mammon."[27] Luke 16:8b appears to have been added as an explanation of 16:8a before the parable came to Luke, for the change to the first person in 16:9 suggests that Luke began to add explanatory comments at that point. This leaves 16:8a as the real problem.

Michaelis[28] and Jeremias[29] regard the parable proper as ending with 16:7, and they take 16:8a to be a genuine reminiscence of the fact that Jesus, as an application and interpretation, praised the dishonest steward; thus *kyrios* in 16:8a refers to Jesus. Jeremias evidently believes, however, that the word *kyrios* is a Lukan addition. These two scholars deny that 16:8a is a part of the parable and that *kyrios* refers to the master in the parable on the ground that the latter would not praise his deceitful servant.

To this it should be said that it seems unlikely that the oral tradition would have preserved an appended statement that Jesus praised a character in his parable. If 16:8a is not an integral part of the parable, it is probably a secondary addition. However, I take it to be an integral part of the parable and *kyrios* to refer to the master in the story. Luke sometimes inserts *ho kyrios* to indicate Jesus' application of a parable, but it is not impossible for the absolute *ho kyrios* to be used of a parabolic character in Luke (cf. 12:37; 12:42b; 14:23); it would seem probable that this is the case in 16:8a since the master has already been referred to as *kyrios* twice in this parable (16:3, 5). As a matter of fact it is not psychologically

[26] Cf. Jeremias, *Parables*, pp. 45–47.
[27] Cf. Michaelis, *Gleichnisse*, pp. 228–229.
[28] *Gleichnisse*, pp. 227–228.
[29] *Parables*, pp. 45–46, 182.

incredible for the master to have praised his deceitful servant,[30] and, as we shall see, the logic of the literary mode to which the parable belongs calls for 16:8a to have been an original part of the parable.

What was originally a parable for the crowds or, more particularly, for Jesus' critics has been turned by Luke into a disciple parable (16:1).

(2) *Literary-existential analysis.* The beginning of the story finds our steward in a crisis. He has been accused before his master of inefficiency or dishonesty and is about to be dismissed. Under the circumstances it would be difficult for him to get another similar position. He was too delicate to dig— or thought that he was—and, not having lost his pride, was ashamed to beg. What was he to do? The fact that he is in danger of being fired rather than punished suggests that he is an employee and not a slave.[31]

The conclusion of part one tells us that the steward has reached a decision about what to do, and the middle part shows him carrying out his resolution. By reducing the amounts owed to his master by his debtors he hoped to win the good will of the debtors—or the general public[32] or both—so that they would take him in when he lost his position. Whether his hopes were to be fulfilled we are not told, but there is at least the implication that his situation was improving in that the ending of the parable relates that the master in some way approved the dishonest steward's actions. Thus we see an internally connected movement from threatening crisis, through decisive response, to an improved situation. The image of man is that of a being who is capable of recognizing that he is in a

[30] Cf. W. O. E. Oesterley, *The Gospel Parables in the Light of Their Jewish Background,* p. 197.

[31] Cf. Michaelis, *Gleichnisse,* p. 226.

[32] Cf. J. Duncan M. Derrett, "Fresh Light on Luke 16," *New Testament Studies,* 7 (1961), 217.

crisis and of laying hold on the situation in such a way as to overcome the threat.

It seems to have been disturbing to some, however, that the crisis resulted from the steward's own misconduct and that he overcame it by more questionable behavior. Attempts have been made to save the steward's character,[33] but these efforts cannot really be brought off. A typical—perhaps correct—interpretation is that the steward was trying to cover up embezzlement by falsifying accounts. The debtors are "tenants who have to deliver a specified portion of the yield" of the land, or they are "merchants who have given promissory notes for goods received." The steward let the debtors alter their notes or make out new ones hoping that, since the changes would be in the same handwriting, his fraud would not be detected.[34] If this is the correct interpretation, then the ending (16:8a) suggests that the master did find out, but being a man of easy standards himself and having some humor and detachment, he praised his steward's ingenuity even though it had cost him something.

A somewhat different interpretation of the parable's economic and legal setting has been given by J. D. M. Derrett, but the steward's character does not come off any better. According to Derrett the steward, as his employer's legal agent, could release debts and the employer would be bound to honor his actions unless he could prove that the agent did not have authority to do this particular thing. The parable assumes that the steward, "doing his worldly duty by his master," has been making usurious loans. It was a typical Jewish practice to liquidate loans and restate them in terms of natural products, thus covering up a usurious transaction. This process made it

---

[33] Cf. J. Alexander Findlay, *Jesus and his Parables*, pp. 81–84; Henry J. Cadbury, "Soluble Difficulties in the Parables," pp. 119–120.

[34] Cf. Jeremias, *Parables*, pp. 181–182; Michaelis, *Gleichnisse*, pp. 226–227.

possible to evade the biblical laws against usury and put the lender legally, but not morally, in the clear. When the steward released a part of the debts, what he did was to cancel the amount that equaled interest plus insurance. The charging of this amount was against the law of God and was oppressive, but, as we have seen, was made legally possible by an accepted subterfuge. In his moment of crisis the steward decided to obey the law of God by canceling the interest and thus to win public approval and acceptance. He believed that his employer would not be so ungracious as to question his right to reduce the debts but would rather want to take credit for the pious acts which he did not initiate. The steward was right in his calculations. Luke 16:8a means not simply that the master praised the steward but that he ratified his reducing of the debts.[35]

In this interpretation the steward has detected that his master is a scheming businessman who wants to make as much money as possible but also wants to appear pious in the eyes of the public. The steward plays upon this defect in his employer and manipulates the latter for his own advantage. Moreover, the fact that the steward's reducing of the debt coincides with the law of God is purely fortuitous. Or more accurately, he purposely does what is pious but purely in the interest of personal advantage—to win public approval—not because of a genuine concern for the well-being of the debtors.

Whatever the exact socio-economic connections of the story, Jesus has placed the action of the steward in an aesthetic configuration which is a miniature of what has come to be known as the picaresque mode. A picaresque comedy tells the story of a successful rogue who makes conventional society look foolish but without establishing any positive alternative.[36] A rogue is one who lives by his wits and partly outside the community's

[35] Derrett, "Luke 16," pp. 203–204, 210, 212, 214, 216–218.
[36] Frye, Anatomy, pp. 45, 229.

standards of responsibility though not in a really threatening
way. He has an acute insight into human responses that may be
played upon to his advantage and is a master of the techniques
for playing upon them. He operates without the inhibitions
created by the community's sense of right and wrong though he
is not so much an enemy of these standards as one who lives in
a different world from them. While his overdeveloped practical
intelligence replaces a full emotional maturity, he is not totally
without feeling. At least he has self-love, and he may experience
fear and disgust and have transient loyalties; but he is not
capable of terror, horror, or hate. Shallowness, and not
criminality, is the key to his character. He secures and plays
on his victim's consent and has a rudimentary rather than a
distorted soul.[37]

The technical problem of securing a measure of sympathy
for the picaresque protagonist may be attacked in various ways.
He may be given certain admired qualities such as a good
nature or charm, or other characters may be given disagreeable
traits. The best method, however, is to keep the victim to a
large extent out of sight in order that he may not usurp sympathy from the *pícaro* (rogue).[38]

The appeal of the typical picaresque work is that by cut-
ting off the larger dimensions of humanity it frees the reader
for a time from moral demands. It gives free play to the tricky,
seamy side of man, a side always present but usually kept
conscientiously under cover, and offers these impulses an opportunity to work themselves off.[39]

That the unjust steward lived beyond the world of communal
norms is seen not only in his questionable business dealings

[37] Cf. Robert B. Heilman, "Variations on Picaresque," *The Sewanee Re-
view*, 66 (1958), 548–550.
[38] *Ibid.*, pp. 551–552.
[39] *Ibid.*, p. 553.

and in his manipulation of his employer and the debtors but also in the fact that he rejected digging and begging, which were very much a part of the regular world of his day. Moreover, he is seen to be fearful about his plight and disgusted at the thought of digging or begging, but he was not terrified. In one way or another he won the approval of his victimized employer. It is this element of success, which belongs to the picaresque mode, that suggests that Luke 16:8a was an original part of the parable.

A degree of sympathy is won for the steward by his trait of at least being candid about his desire for an easy life. The fact that the employer is characterized as "rich" may suggest that he, too, is a schemer; and if it is correct to see the steward as dealing in usurious loans, this activity is certainly at the behest of his employer. Moreover, the latter is kept to a large extent out of sight.

The Unjust Steward's exemplification of the picaresque mode means that it produces the typically picaresque aesthetic experience referred to above.

(3) *Existential-theological interpretation.* The parable in itself says that the present is a crisis because the future is threatening, and the comic form in which the story is cast suggests that man by making an appropriate response to the crisis can overcome the danger. But this is all configured in the picaresque mode with its "moral holiday" as well as its catharsis of the seamy side of man.

The crisis note in the parable points subsidiarily to the same theme in Jesus' non-parabolic eschatological preaching (Luke 12:8-9; Mark 8:38; Luke 17:22-30) with its offer of unconditional acceptance (cf. Mark 2:15-17) and its demand for unconditional obedience (cf. Matt. 5:21-48). But because the parable is an aesthetic object which has its meaning and its power to grasp and inform the attention through its total configuration, one cannot simply isolate for consideration the point or points of contact with Jesus' non-parabolic teaching and ignore the points of tension. There is, as noted, a positive correlation between the crisis theme in the parable and in Jesus' non-parabolic teaching, and the catharsis element is certainly not inimical to Jesus' message. But the character of the unjust steward, along with its aesthetic effect, hardly accords with Jesus' demand for self-denial and for unlimited purity and love. Is it too much to say that this tension places in Jesus' message as a whole at least an element of comic relief from dead seriousness, as the parable with a happy earthiness offers our tricky side a temporary aesthetic fling? And perhaps the more profound theological implication of this aesthetic effect is that our well-being does not rest ultimately on our dead seriousness.

3. *The Prodigal Son* (Luke 15:11-32)

[11]And he said, "There was a man who had two sons; [12]and the younger of them said to his father, 'Father, give me the share of property that falls to me.' And he divided his living between them. [13]Not many days later, the younger son gathered all he had and took his journey into a far country, and there he squandered his property in loose living. [14]And when he had spent everything, a great famine arose in that country, and he began to be in want. [15]So he went and joined himself to one of the citizens of that country, who sent him into his fields to feed swine. [16]And he would gladly have fed on the pods that the swine ate; and no one gave him anything. [17]But when he came to himself he said, 'How many of my father's hired servants have bread enough and to spare, but I perish here with hunger! [18]I will arise and go to my father, and I will say to him, "Father, I have sinned against heaven and before you; [19]I am no longer worthy to be called your son; treat me as one of your hired servants." ' [20]And he arose and came to his father. But while he was yet at a distance, his father saw him and had compassion, and ran and embraced him and kissed him. [21]And the son said to him, 'Father, I have sinned against heaven and before you; I am no longer worthy to be called your son.' [22]But the father said to his servants, 'Bring

162

quickly the best robe, and put it on him; and put a ring on his hand, and shoes on his feet; [28]and bring the fatted calf and kill it, and let us eat and make merry; [24]for this my son was dead, and is alive again; he was lost, and is found.' And they began to make merry.

[25]"Now his elder son was in the field; and as he came and drew near to the house, he heard music and dancing. [26]And he called one of the servants and asked what this meant. [27]And he said to him, 'Your brother has come, and your father has killed the fatted calf, because he has received him safe and sound.' [28]But he was angry and refused to go in. His father came out and entreated him, [29]but he answered his father, 'Lo, these many years I have served you, and I never disobeyed your command; yet you never gave me a kid, that I might make merry with my friends [30]But when this son of yours came, who has devoured your living with harlots, you killed for him the fatted calf!' [31]And he said to him, 'Son, you are always with me, and all that is mine is yours. [32]It was fitting to make merry and be glad, for this your brother was dead, and is alive; he was lost, and is found.' "

(1) *Historico-literary criticism.* The Prodigal Son naturally comes last, as a climax to the interpretation of the several parables, not simply because it is the longest of Jesus' extant parables and probably has been the most influential on the mind of the church and of Western man as a whole, but because from the standpoint of both theme and plot it is the most complex and inclusive.

The elder brother section is to be considered a genuine and original part of the parable. In view of a parable's characteristic economy, there would probably have been no mention of *two* sons in the first part (15:11-12) had there been no intention to bring both of them into the story. Moreover, in its contrasting of two human types The Prodigal Son is similar to such parables as The Two Sons (Matt. 21:28-31).[40] In addition the elder brother part reflects Jesus' historical situation

[40] Cf. Rudolf Bultmann, *The History of the Synoptic Tradition,* p. 196; Jeremias, *Parables,* p. 131; Linnemann, *Gleichnisse,* p. 84.

and apart from this probably would not have been included,[41] since the parable is aesthetically satisfactory without it.

That is to say, the elder brother in some sense represents the scribes and Pharisees, who protested Jesus' fellowship with the publicans and sinners, who in some sense are represented by the prodigal.[42] But the parable is not an allegory,[43] for the patterns of connection are primarily internal and centripetal.

(2) *Literary-existential analysis*. It has often been claimed that the father is the central figure in the parable[44] and even that this is true to such an extent that it should be called The Father's Love.[45] But it may be rejoined that the instinct of the Christian and Western tradition has been right in calling it The Prodigal Son, for it is the son's story. His experience gives the plot its formal shape. Moreover, in all of the other narrative parables (with the possible exception of The Ten Maidens) the master figure in some way initiates or evokes the action even though his experience does not give the plot its structure. But in The Prodigal Son the son not only gives the plot its structure but also initiates the action. As in The Unforgiving Servant, we have a double plot movement, but in The Prodigal Son it is the opposite of the movement in the former parable. That is, the prodigal's fortune changes from good to bad to good.

The beginning of the story finds the son in what was apparently a satisfactory home situation. At least it was good enough to draw him back later. The young man, however, wanted to strike out on his own; therefore, he prevailed upon his father to give him that part of the inheritance which was

---

[41] Cf. A. T. Cadoux, *The Parables of Jesus*, p. 121.

[42] Cf. Linnemann, *Gleichnisse*, pp. 79–80; Jeremias, *Parables*, pp. 131–132; Michaelis, *Gleichnisse*, p. 143.

[43] As is claimed by Matthew Black, "The Parables as Allegory," p. 284.

[44] Cf. Günther Bornkamm, *Jesus of Nazareth*, p. 126.

[45] Jeremias, *Parables*, p. 128.

due him, and turning his share of the property into liquid assets, he left home.

In the middle part we see how the prodigal lived out his decision. He quickly spent his money in loose living and was reduced to poverty and despair. But he came to some self-knowledge and resolved to return home, hoping at best to be received as a servant.

In the ending his father welcomed him, most surprisingly, with all of the tokens of restored sonship and called for the preparation of a feast of rejoicing. That the establishment of a renewed society should be "signalized by some kind of party or festive ritual" is typical of the comic ending.[46] As a matter of fact, eating imagery is used to represent both of the prodigal's opposite extremities, and hence his rescue or redemption is suggested by the contrasting eating images. In the depths of his poverty he is hungry; and the carob pods which he would have eaten, had anyone given him some, were generally used as fodder for animals. Only in great poverty would humans eat them. Hence the rabbis said: "When the Israelites are reduced to eating carob-pods, then they repent."[47] Upon the prodigal's return, however, the fatted calf is killed for him.

We see in The Prodigal Son a plot structure of interlocking parts moving finally upward from decision, through dissolution, to well-being and restoration. If the comic and hopeful may be lost in tragedy (The Unforgiving Servant), it is also possible for the tragic to be overcome by comedy (The Prodigal Son).

Frye[48] has pointed out that the form of comedy may be developed in two ways: (a) The main emphasis may be placed on blocking characters, characters who resist the comic movement of the hero's story. (b) The accent may be caused to fall

---

[46] Frye, *Anatomy*, p. 163.
[47] Quoted from Manson, *Sayings*, p. 288.
[48] *Anatomy*, pp. 166–167.

165

on scenes of discovery and reconciliation. The blocking character is typically made absurd by attributing to him some ruling passion. The plot movement is usually from a society controlled by habit, bondage, or law—a society typical of the blocking character—to a society marked by freedom.[49]

The Prodigal Son reflects these characteristic features of comedy but with its own modifications. The elder brother— the blocking character—is given a certain stress by the fact that the section dealing with him comes last; nevertheless, the discovery and reconciliation of the prodigal are more fully and powerfully developed than is the elder brother's story, and the treatment of the theme (cf. below) also puts the emphasis on the prodigal's redemption. The elder brother, however, is too realistically like us to be absurd in the sense meant by Frye.

The plot does not present a movement from a society dominated by law—a society which would be typical of the elder brother's outlook—but rather a movement from irresponsibility on the part of the prodigal to a new contextual freedom. In the ending the prodigal is free from want and free from law, that is, free from the need to establish his position through his own efforts. But the father-son relationship is restored, and such a context, such a relationship, imposes responsibility as well as offers freedom. As Tillich has pointed out, there is no freedom without destiny, without a context of concrete alternatives among which one chooses, nor is there freedom without responsibility, without being willing to answer for one's choices.[50] The elder brother's story is a kind of separate chapter which makes the contrast between law (the elder brother part) and contextual freedom (the ending of the prodigal's story) run parallel, so to speak, to the contrast between irresponsibility

[49] *Ibid.*, pp. 168–169.
[50] Paul Tillich, *Systematic Theology*, Vol. 1 (Chicago: University of Chicago Press, 1953), pp. 202–204.

and contextual freedom. We have this parallelism rather than having the society of law worked into the plot texture of the prodigal's story. While the elder brother is a blocking character, there is also a sense in which the prodigal is his own blocking character. It is his abuse of freedom which produces his dissolution and the threat to his existence. Thus we see the influence of the biblical understanding of sin on the comic mode.

From the standpoint of plot The Prodigal Son has a rounded and complete beginning, middle, and end without the elder brother episode; but we saw above that there are good reasons for considering the latter an original part of the parable. Moreover, the elder brother chapter is brought within the thematic unity of the prodigal's story. How the elder brother responded to his father's entreaty to come in to the festival is not related. Rather the elder brother episode—and hence the whole parable—is concluded by the father's repeating (15:32) the statement which he uttered at the end of the prodigal's story (15:24) and which expresses the movement and meaning of the latter. Thus the main interest of the story as a whole is seen to be the redemption of the prodigal.

As we noted in the chapter on the tragic parables, the sequence of events in those stories is tragic action, recognition scene, downfall. In The Prodigal Son, on the other hand, it is tragic action (squandering his money and loose living), downfall (his reduction to poverty and degradation), recognition scene. In the tragic parables the recognition scene—if there is to be one at all—must come before the downfall since the ending (downfall) is something after which there is nothing. But The Prodigal Son is a comedy which includes and overcomes tragedy; therefore, the recognition scene follows the downfall as the most appropriate transition to the comic rescue of the tragic. In the comic ending the recognition scene is taken up again and transcended. That is, the prodigal acknowledged to

167

his father, as he had acknowledged to himself, the forfeiture of his sonship, but the father took him back as son. And in The Prodigal Son, as in the tragic parables, the recognition scene is still after the initiating action, indicating the blindness with which man acts according to the biblical view of things.

In the recognition scene the prodigal is seen to be aware of his physical destitution and also of his having sinned against God and his father. It is not altogether clear, however, whether he meant by his sinfulness only his loose and wasteful living or also included in his sinning his leaving home in the first place. In any case he believed that he had destroyed his relationship with his father and forfeited the right of sonship. The prodigal did not blame someone else or the nature of life itself for his plight but rather accused himself and assumed responsibility for his situation. As the rest of the story shows, however, what he accused was not an unalterable essence but an aspect of himself, a forgivable aspect. There are still meaningful possibilities to be realized after confession and self-accusation.

The recognition scene presents man as capable of "coming to himself," and a part of this is the recollection of one's past. The son's confession is to some extent awakened by the memory of his father and his home.[51] Man is seen as capable of recognizing who and where he is, particularly of knowing that something is wrong. This image of man provides a clear contrast with those moderns whom Karl Heim[52] would call the thoroughgoing secularists. The semi-secularist may assert that life is painful and meaningless, but he is still protesting this state of affairs. He agrees with the prodigal at least in recognizing that something is wrong. The thoroughgoing secularist, on the

[51] Cf. Bornkamm, *Jesus*, pp. 126–127.
[52] *Christian Faith and Natural Science*, trans. N. H. Smith (London: SCM Press, 1953), pp. 17–19.

other hand, has come to accept the normalcy of hell. He has given up the illusion that life ought to be meaningful and therefore has no protest to make. The loss of meaning is not wrong but rather normal.

The prodigal is able not only to recognize that something is wrong but to resolve to do something about it. The total movement of the story reveals, however, that more can be done about it than he can imagine. The final help comes from beyond him and far exceeds his expectations. He is incapable of knowing what possibilities for good might come to him until they do come.

The question of how the parable represents the prodigal's sin depends somewhat on the nature of the young man's leave-taking. Some interpreters see the latter as a self-assertive and autonomous repudiation of the father's influence; thus leaving home itself would have produced estrangement.[53] In Bornkamm's view the son has despised goodness and treated his father "as if he were already dead."[54] This interpretation would seem to depend on the view that *normally* a son could acquire legal possession of his share of the inheritance during his father's lifetime but not the right to dispose of it until his father's death.[55] The right of disposal could indeed be obtained, though to do so was to demand a special privilege.[56] Thus the prodigal's demand for the right of disposal was to treat his father as if he were dead.

In Linnemann's view, on the other hand, it was not unusual that the younger son of a comfortably well-off peasant should ask his father for his share of the inheritance. To Jesus' audi-

[53] Cf. Manson, *Sayings*, p. 288; Geraint V. Jones, *The Art and Truth of the Parables*, pp. 175, 184, 185, 197.

[54] Bornkamm, *Jesus*, pp. 126–127.

[55] Cf. Herbert Danby, *The Mishnah* (Oxford University Press, 1933), p. 377.

[56] Apparently the view of Manson, *Sayings*, pp. 287–288; Jeremias, *Parables*, pp. 128–129.

ence the younger son's petition would sound like a legitimate
request and not like an insolent demand.[57] Indeed, according
to Michaelis, the son may be represented as at first an especially
industrious young man who wanted to make a life of his own
abroad.[58] The situation may be somewhat clarified if we accept
Smith's view that the law forbidding a son to sell property
given to him by his father during the latter's lifetime was not
yet in force in Jesus' time.[59] If this is the correct interpretation of the legal and social situation, then the leave-taking
itself might not represent an autonomous breaking out of the
personal. The son's sin is rather his wasteful mode of life.
He became an unworthy son through the wanton irresponsibility with which he dissipated his father's living, which had
been freely given to him.

It has been suggested that for Jesus sin is being "in the
wrong place,"[60] and this certainly applies to the prodigal. He
was hungry among the swine in a foreign country when he
could have been in his father's house where even the servants
had plenty to eat. But is his being in the wrong place the fact
that he had left home at all or is it the place he had got himself
into after an innocent leave-taking? Clearly his going home is a
redemption. Does this suggest, then, that leaving home was in
some sense a fall? Moreover, while it may have been quite
legal for the son to seek and to receive the right of disposal
of his share of the inheritance, at least some Jewish circles
frowned on a father's giving complete control of some portion
of his property to his children before his death (Ecclus. 33:19-
23). It is difficult to believe that the parable places no judg-

---

[57] Cf. Linnemann, *Gleichnisse*, pp. 80–81. According to Linnemann the
younger of two sons was entitled to one-third of the disposable property but
not to any of the real estate.

[58] Michaelis, *Gleichnisse*, p. 138.

[59] Smith, *Parables*, pp. 194–195.

[60] Gerhard Gloege, *The Day of His Coming*, trans. S. Rudman (Philadelphia: Fortress Press, 1963), p. 180.

ment at all on the leave-taking as such though the emphasis may well be on the son's irresponsible squandering of his money with harlots.

This is probably a good place to deal with the flaw of the elder brother. The view that the parable does not put him in a bad light[61] seems doubtful. He, too, is in the wrong place, for not only is he outside of the house where the music and dancing are—is there a hint that he disapproves of music and dancing?—but he willfully remains outside. His resentment over the fact that his wayward brother had been royally welcomed home while his own consistent obedience had not been re- warded with merrymaking does not suggest that he is a self- righteous man who has cancelled his previous righteousness by his present lovelessness.[62] The older son revealed, rather, that his obedience had always been based on a misunderstanding. His belief that his relationship with his father was based on merit and reward stood in the way of a deeply personal rela- tionship. He complained that his father had never even given him a kid to celebrate with—when all of the time all that his father had was his. He, however, was incapable of knowing this at the level of immediate, personal engagement.

The ending of the prodigal's story restores the father-son relationship and is truly a new beginning, a new beginning based on the surprising generosity of the father rather than on the merits of the son. The acceptance is not based on any con- ditions, probation, or proofs of repentance. In fact repentance finally turns out to be the capacity to forego pride and accept graciousness. It should be noticed that the father not only goes out to the prodigal son; he also goes out to the elder brother.

As has been noted, the thematic meaning of the parable is expressed by the father both at the end of the prodigal's story and at the end of the elder brother episode: the lost

[61] As is claimed by Smith, *Parables*, p. 194.
[62] As Michaelis holds, *Gleichnisse*, p. 143.

has been found; he who was dead is alive. The issues involved could not be more crucial, for the question of life or death is at stake. The difference between holding oneself answerable to no one and being graciously received into a context where acceptance need not be earned but where one is answerable for deciding between real alternatives is the difference between death and life. The difference between believing that one must merit acceptance and being graciously accepted into a situation of freedom-and-responsibility is also the difference between death and life.

One of the typical heroes of twentieth-century fiction is the figure whom R. W. B. Lewis calls the "picaresque saint." By taking on sinfulness and wretchedness he experiences fellowship with the suffering human race. He tries to keep in balance, just in the contradictions of his character, both the observed truths of contemporary experience and the intense desire to move beyond them. Although he is an outsider, he is an outsider who gains entrance, and he usually experiences a conversion from something like death to something like life.[63] The prodigal son's kinship with the picaresque saint is obvious.

(3) *Existential-theological interpretation.* The father's surprising but not impossible actions cut across the everyday way of looking at things and point to God. It was generally beneath the dignity of an older oriental to run,[64] but this father ran to his returning son. Moreover, his actions might be taken as indulgent, for he risked encouraging the prodigal in his profligacy; he also risked offending his older son,[65] but he took these risks. The pointing to God, however, is both subsidiary and indirect because Jesus was defending first his own gracious association with sinners. Yet he wanted his conduct to be understood as

---

[63] Cf. Lewis, *Picaresque*, pp. 28, 31, 33.
[64] Cf. Linnemann, *Gleichnisse*, p. 83.
[65] Cf. Findlay, *Parables*, p. 73; Fuchs, *Historical Jesus*, pp. 20, 160–161.

explaining the will of God.[66] The father in the parable, then, points subsidiarily both to Jesus' historical conduct and to the nature of God.

According to Manson[67] the parable lays down the fundamental principle that God loves the sinner before he repents and that somehow the divine love makes repentance possible. This position may well be true if we understand by repentance the total movement of the son from his coming to himself, through his return home, to his own acceptance of his father's gracious reception of him. But it does not seem to recognize that the self-understanding of the son at the time of his coming to himself is different from that which he has later, after he has actually been welcomed. There is a late rabbinic parable in which the father says: "Come as far as you can, my son, and I will come the rest of the way."[68] Neither does this parable express the change in self-understanding which is suggested by The Prodigal Son, and the rabbinic parable implies that the movements of father and son—God and man—are on the same plane.

The Prodigal Son, by suggesting a radical change in the self-understanding of the prodigal, implies that something has come to him from a different dimension. His coming to himself suggests that natural man can be aware of guilt and of the need for the restoration of fellowship with God, but he understands this in terms of law. The prodigal hopes that law will be tinged with mercy, for he does hope that his father will receive him back as a servant. But his understanding is basically oriented to law. He has forfeited the right of sonship and does not expect it back. That is to say, natural man does not know God as the one who forgives radically and does not know himself as accepted in spite of his unacceptability. As Bultmann has

---

[66] Fuchs, *Historical Jesus*, pp. 20, 25.
[67] *Sayings*, p. 286.
[68] Quoted from Findlay, *Parables*, p. 74. Findlay does not give his source.

said, for natural man God is remote, and sonship is experienced as a judgment.[69]

The prodigal son knows his father as the gracious person he really is and knows himself as a son again—and not a servant—only when he is actually received back. Only when the event of forgiveness occurred and shattered his own view of things did his understanding change. The son did take the initiative to come back, but the situation into which he came was qualitatively different, of a different dimension, from what he expected. This suggests that natural man's legalistic understanding of the divine-human relationship is shattered only by the unexpected event of forgiveness which comes to him from beyond himself. Thus we may say with Bornkamm[70] that The Prodigal Son makes clear that the fatherhood of God can be understood only as an event which now happens, as a miracle. When God is known as forgiver, he is near and no longer remote.[71]

The comic movement of The Prodigal Son is from well-being, through fall, back to well-being, and this is also true for the total sweep of the Bible—from Genesis to Revelation. But if this movement is referred to as cyclical,[72] it should not be thought that either the Bible in general or The Prodigal Son in particular envisions a literal cyclical return to the same beginning. In the strictly cyclical view of time everything is fixed in the *Urzeit*, and nothing really new can happen. While the biblical view of time cannot be simply represented by a solid straight line, and while there are recurring patterns in the biblical picture, it is still true that in the latter the new does emerge, and the *Endzeit* is not identical with the *Urzeit*.[73]

[69] Bultmann, *Jesus and the Word*, p. 194.
[70] *Jesus*, p. 128.
[71] Bultmann, *Theology of the New Testament*, Vol. 1, p. 24.
[72] As it is by Frye, *Anatomy*, pp. 171, 316.
[73] Cf. Brevard S. Childs, *Myth and Reality in the Old Testament* ("Studies in Biblical Theology," No. 27 [London: SCM Press, 1960]), pp. 73–83.

There are both continuity and discontinuity, and this is also true for the existence of the prodigal son. At the end he was the same person that he was at the beginning, and yet not quite. Throughout his story possibilities became actualized which had been only potentialities. In The Prodigal Son, and characteristically in the Bible, past, present, and future are distinct—and thus real—though interrelated.

Ebeling's interpretation of existence in faith puts the emphasis on the future and makes the present little more than the transition from the remembered past to the all important future.[74] Fuchs, on the other hand gives more substance to the present. It is the time of the called while the future is God's time for which man could and should do nothing. The result is that "calling means being free for" and "within the bounds of the present."[75] As we have seen, Fuchs' view is supported by such parables as The Talents and The Ten Maidens. In The Prodigal Son, however, the emphasis is somewhat different.

In The Ten Maidens, for example, the present is determined by a future expectation. From the beginning the young women are consciously aware of a definite, expected future event, and they orient their actions in the light of it with the result that their different ways of conducting themselves affect their future destinies. In The Prodigal Son, on the other hand, the young man's actions are determined largely by his intentions about or his response to his immediate, present situation. Thus we see a kind of present developing in its own immediacy, a present which takes its content from itself, rather than from an expectation about or the impingement of the future. In the beginning there is no indication that the son initiates the action because of a future expectation. It is rather in response to the call of the here and now that he acts. In his recognition scene he does hope that in the future his father will take him

[74] Gerhard Ebeling, *Word and Faith*, pp. 214–215, 240–241.
[75] Fuchs, *Historical Jesus*, p. 163.

175

back as a servant, and he also remembers his past, but the emphasis in his coming to himself is his interpretation of the fact that he is a swineherd in the present. In the richly filled present of the ending the father's welcoming and joyous activities are in response to an unexpected present.

This does not mean that the story is not aware of the difference between past, present, and future—for it clearly is— and it does not portray an eternal present. It is simply that at any moment the actions and recognitions occur as a response to or an intention about the present rather than as a response to an expected future event. Thus in The Prodigal Son the present is given an immediacy and a significance in itself which it does not have in such parables as The Ten Maidens and The Talents.

6

The Parables, the Gospels, and the Historical Jesus

Heretofore we have discussed a number of the parables primarily, though not exclusively, as individual units. This has been justified because these stories, as aesthetic objects, have a certain autonomy and because this is the way they would have confronted Jesus' hearers. While the first hearers of the parables would have had varying degrees of knowledge about Jesus' actions and teachings, they would have been in no position to see them in the light of Jesus' whole history and obviously could not have seen them in the light of the structure of the Gospels in which they came to be included. We, however, can and do see the parables in connection with Jesus' history—as sketchy as it is—and in connection with the Synoptic Gospels. Some attention must therefore be given to the parables' relationship to these two complexes. To consider the parables in relation to the individual theologies of the Synoptic evangelists would take us too far afield; hence the discussion of the Gospels will be limited chiefly to the relationship of the parables in general to what might be called the Gospel form.

1. The Form of the Parables and the Form of the Gospels

It is a commonplace of contemporary theology that the Gospels are kerygmatic. Their form and framework are deter-

mined by theological concerns, by the Easter faith. At the same
time they identify the risen Christ with the historical Jesus,
and whether or not they were intended as historical sources—
and we must consider below whether they were so intended—
to some extent they still serve as such.[1] It may be true that the
Gospels' unique combination of a historical event with an interpretation of that event which sees it as the final manifestation of the transcendent distinguishes the Gospels from any
category in the history of ancient literature.[2] Or it may be said
similarly that the Gospel is the only wholly new form created
by the church.[3] It is not impossible, however, to indicate the
Gospels' affinities with other literary types. But before doing
that it is necessary to consider the relationship of the parables
to the Gospels in a general and theoretical way.

It will be recalled that, according to Polanyi, in genuine
understanding focal attention is on a gestalt or configuration,
while the particulars that make up the larger complex receive
only subsidiary attention. Moreover, a particular is truly known
only when seen in the light of its most comprehensive context.[4]
If we apply this principle to the Gospels, then we must say
that although from the standpoint of the situations in which
Jesus told the parables the parables themselves were the focus,
now that they have been included in a more comprehensive
literary structure, that new structure has become the focus and
the parables are subsidiary. To make the parables subsidiary
to the larger story of Jesus and to the kerygmatic interpretation
of that story was certainly the intention of the evangelists, and
to the extent that their intention can be carried out the par-

[1] Cf. Hans Werner Bartsch, "The Historical Problem of the Life of Jesus,"
in The Historical Jesus and the Kerygmatic Christ, p. 116; Hans Conzelmann, "The Method of the Life of Jesus Research," in The Historical Jesus
and the Kerygmatic Christ, p. 57.

[2] Cf. Günther Bornkamm, in Tradition and Interpretation in Matthew,
p. 52.

[3] Amos N. Wilder, Early Christian Rhetoric, pp. 36–37.

[4] Michael Polanyi, The Study of Man, pp. 52, 71.

ables become vehicles for the expression of the whole kerygmatic meaning of the Gospels. When a parable is seen in the light of the larger whole, it gathers the whole into itself.

We must, however, raise the question whether the evangelists actually are able to carry out their intention to make the parables subsidiary to the structure of the Gospels. It is my judgment that the parables—because they are aesthetic objects, because of their organic interlocking of form-and-content—resist the effort to assimilate them to the form of the Gospels in a way that the other materials used by the evangelists do not. Some resistance is offered also by other units which have achieved a certain fullness of form, such as miracle stories and apothegms. The latter, however, have Jesus as their central character, just as he is in the Gospel story as a whole; therefore, they do not in any far-reaching way deflect attention from the overall structure of the Gospels. The parables, on the other hand, have their own characters and their own autonomous world with the result that they cannot become merely subsidiary to the structure of the Gospels but rather contend inevitably with the latter for the focal attention of the reader. Thus the parables make a claim to be a clue to the meaning of the Gospels as well as derive a part of their meaning—in their present position—from the Gospels. The reader who becomes deeply and personally involved in the reading of the Gospels is caught in a kind of tension and/or movement between the form of the Gospel and the form of the parables.

What, then, more precisely, is the form of the Gospels? To debate the question of whether or not the Gospel form should be called a definite literary genre[5] would not be as fruitful as

[5] Ernst Fuchs (*Studies of the Historical Jesus*, p. 66) holds that the Gospels are a new genre which should not be called "minor literature." Rudolf Bultmann (*The History of the Synoptic Tradition*, pp. 373–374), on the other hand, holds that while the Gospel form was capable of development, canonization prevented that development from taking place (except for John's modification of Mark); therefore, it is not proper to speak of the Gospels as a literary genre.

to consider concretely its kinship with and differences from the Western literary tradition. In the Gospels we see Jesus seeking and intending to bring to men the gracious presence and rule of God, but his efforts resulted in conflict and finally in his death. On the cross he suffered the tragic recognition that his good purpose had produced forsakenness by God. The resurrection, however, shows that he was not really abandoned, although he believed that he was, and proves his death to have been in truth a victory. From the standpoint of plot, then, the Gospel form might be called the tragedy of an innocent sufferer which is followed by a post-tragic redemptive episode[6] or, similarly, a tragedy which paradoxically includes victory.[7] In view of the emphasis which the Gospels clearly put on the resurrection, however, it seems more appropriate to speak of the Gospel form as a comedy in which the tragic is included and overcome.[8] The ease and appropriateness with which the categories of tragedy and comedy can be used of the Gospels manifest their affinity with the literary tradition.

From the standpoint of Frye's classification of protagonists according to their power of action, the Gospels appear to be, and to an extent are, myths, for Jesus in the Gospel picture is superior in kind to other men and to the environment. The evangelists present him as the eschatological figure who in some sense shares the nature of God. That, however, is only a part of the story. Jesus is presented as a real, human figure of the recent past, a carpenter (or son of a carpenter) who became a teacher and was at the mercy of other men who did him to death. This combination of features, however, does not make the Gospels what Frye calls "displaced myth." In this genre the protagonist is a human being who is simply associated with a reality—like the sun—which in a real myth would

---

[6] Oscar Mandel, A Definition of Tragedy, pp. 113–115.
[7] Northrop Frye, Anatomy of Criticism, p. 220.
[8] Cf. ibid., p. 215.

180

be deified and with which the protagonist would be identified.[9] In the Gospels, on the other hand, Jesus is not simply associated with God. Jesus' life *is* the divine action though he is finite and mortal. This interlacing of the mythological and the realistic, of the divine and the human, defies classification according to the categories of ancient literature.

We might say that the Gospel form is the tragicomedy of the God-man which proclaims and offers to other men the comic overcoming of their tragic loss of existence.

In considering the relationship of the parables to the Gospels it may be recalled that it is typical of the parables to have a master-father figure, who usually evokes the action, and a servant-subject-son figure, whose story gives the parable its formal shape. These two figures are clearly distinguished, but in the Gospels this distinction is moderated. Jesus, as the instrument of the eschatological rule of God, is the master who calls men to radical obedience and to follow in his way. But he is also the servant-subject figure whose story gives the Gospels their formal structure. As the servant of God he suffers in obedience, and by being the servant of God he is also the servant of men in that men do with him as they will and also in the sense that his death paradoxically is for their redemption. Jesus' resurrection demonstrates that the man who loses his life—who in freedom risks self-contrived security—gains his life. Whoever reads the parables as a part of the Gospels is to understand himself in between the servant-subject figure of the parables and the master-servant of the Gospels. The parables keep the reader anchored in the everyday world, although it is a world also mysteriously crossed by the unexpected, and show him what his possibilities are in that world. The Gospels show him the ground of those possibilities, a ground only allusively and subsidiarily suggested in the parables.

[9] *Ibid.*, p. 137.

Jesus' call to men creates a crisis of decision. A person must decide what to do with his life or what he will let be done with it. The tragic parables reveal what is involved in deciding against the eschatological act of God. When they are read in juxtaposition with the Gospel story, the effect is tension, for we are made to realize that while the ultimate meaning of life is comic—the form of the Gospels—the meaning of an individual life may be tragic—the form of the tragic parables. Authentic existence has been decisively revealed in Jesus' life, but men may still lose their existence.

We may recall that the plot movement of The Prodigal Son is from well-being, through suffering and despair, to new life won from death. The plot movement of the Gospels is also from well-being, through suffering and a sense of abandonment, to the victory of life over death. There is an overall parallelism here but also tension. The man who lets his existence be informed by the structures of The Prodigal Son and the story of Jesus will know that while Jesus' suffering and death resulted from his intention to bring the presence of God, his own suffering and despair, like the prodigal's, are the consequence of wanton irresponsibility and self-concern. But there is movement as well, for the life (resurrection) which issued from Jesus' innocent death has the power to take the death born of sin into itself and turn it into new life. The man who is taken from death to life by Jesus' story participates, in his own way, in the same kind of risky renunciation of security which Jesus accepted. He gives up both the prideful attempt to establish himself with God by his own efforts and the inverted pride of unrelenting self-condemnation.

2. The Parables and Eschatology

In the preceding section the Gospels were treated primarily as literary pieces, as aesthetic objects. This was justified by

182

their affinities with the Western literary tradition, and such an approach can tell us a good deal about their meaning and effect. The Gospels, however, are not by any means aesthetic to the extent that the parables are. The latter are imaginative creations which point only subsidiarily and indirectly, by analogy, to Jesus' historical situation. The Gospels, on the other hand, point directly to Jesus, and it cannot have been a matter of indifference to the evangelists whether or not Jesus lived. It is a part of the content which they inform in their kerygmatic structure that the eschatological act of God occurred in a particular history, and they give us a history of Jesus, however disconnected, episodic, and theologically arranged it may be. Because of the New Testament view that revelation occurred in a particular history it also makes a difference what Jesus did and how he understood it, although it would be impossible to say how much of this content needs to be known.

The line of distinction between Jesus and the kerygma is not unambiguous, and it will always remain problematical whether certain elements reflect the historical Jesus or the kerygma, yet some distinctions can be made. This does not mean, however, that Jesus' story as distinguished from the kerygmatic framework of the Gospels is uninterpreted fact. It also has its pattern of meaning. The parables, therefore, need to be seen in relation to the pattern of connections in Jesus' story as well as in relation to the pattern of connections in the finished kerygmatic Gospel.

The effort to uncover as much as possible of the historical Jesus' interpretation of his mission may rest on the theological assumption that there is something uniquely authoritative for the Christian faith in the historical Jesus.[10] The effort may also rest on the historiographical consideration that every epoch

[10] Cf. Joachim Jeremias, *The Parables of Jesus*, pp. 9, 114; Gerhard Gloege, *The Day of His Coming*, p. 7.

is centered on itself and should be interpreted in the light of its own pattern of connections.[11] Thus the epochs of Jesus and of the early church should be distinguished. One is inclined to agree with Van Buren that if historical research could show that Jesus made an agreement with the authorities to stay in the wilderness and let someone else be crucified in his place, thus revealing that he was as insecure and self-interested as anyone else, the Christian faith as the New Testament presents it would be untenable. In this sense faith is based on history, and if this puts faith at the mercy of the historian, that is the inevitable risk of centering Christianity on a historical figure.[12]

If, on the other hand, it could be proved by historical scholarship—which it could not—that Jesus was perfectly secure and without self-interest, it would still not legitimate the kerygma. Because the New Testament proclaims that God acted finally in Jesus' history—because the New Testament is concerned with both history and the transcendent—faith is both interested and uninterested in historical questions.[13] To show that there is a basic consistency between the kerygma's and Jesus' understanding of existence would not prove that the transcendent really had entered into time; moreover, the demonstration of consistency would not relieve one of the risks involved in making this understanding of existence one's own. However, if it could be shown that there is a basic inconsistency between Jesus' and the kerygma's understanding of existence, one might legitimately question the validity of the kerygma or Jesus or both. On this negative side historical questions cannot be ignored.

[11] Wilhelm Dilthey, *Pattern and Meaning in History*, pp. 129–131.

[12] Paul Van Buren, *The Secular Meaning of the Gospel*, pp. 125–126.

[13] Cf. Hermann Diem, "The Earthly Jesus and the Christ of Faith," in *Kerygma and History*, ed. and trans. C. E. Braaten and R. A. Harrisville (New York and Nashville: Abingdon Press, 1962), p. 205; Nils A. Dahl, "The Problem of the Historical Jesus," in *Kerygma and History*, pp. 159–171; Hugh Anderson, *Jesus and Christian Origins*, p. 116.

Let it be agreed that the decision of faith in a sense is free of historical considerations. This assertion is true, however, only of the first moment of faith and of certain other moments of faith. When we go on to consider faith as the stance of the whole man lived as a process, then we recognize that this man, who reasons as well as wills and feels, *will* ask about such things as the continuity between Jesus' preaching and the kerygma. If faith cannot justify itself intellectually—through theologizing—there will be a split between the intellectual, on the one hand, and, on the other, the volitional and emotive, which are more prominent in faith. Thus a historical-critical-theological concern with the continuity between Jesus and the kerygma is called for by the need to live a unified existence. Repeated unquestioning responses interlaced with continuing theological reflection would be part of the ongoing dialectic of the Christian life.

It is widely agreed and seems reasonably certain that the central theme in the preaching of the historical Jesus was the kingdom or rule of God.[14] It is highly probable, moreover, that Jesus' proclamation of the future kingdom was apocalyptic in nature. To be sure Jesus did reject the calculating of the exact time of the end by observing signs (Luke 17:20 ff.)[15] and had no interest in fanciful descriptions of the new world, but he retained the apocalyptic expectation of a cosmic catastrophe in the near future which would involve the disappearance of

---

[14] Fuchs at times seems to deny that the kingdom itself made up the content of Jesus' preaching (*Historical Jesus*, p. 143), though he holds that Jesus pondered the problem of the kingdom and expressed himself on it (*ibid.*, p. 179). Probably Fuchs' hesitation about saying that Jesus directly proclaimed the coming of the kingdom stems from his desire to avoid reducing Jesus' message to the proclamation of the end of time (*ibid.*, pp. 108, 111, 112, 116).

[15] But N. A. Dahl has shown that although for Jesus the final day will come suddenly and unexpectedly, Jesus nevertheless believed that by divine necessity certain things had to happen before the end ("The Parables of Growth," p. 146).

this world and the advent of a new one.[16] At the same time
Jesus proclaimed that the kingdom of God was eschatologically
—decisively—present in his ministry. There are individual sayings which make the kingdom eschatologically future (Mark
8:38; 13:28-29) and individual sayings which make it eschatologically present (Matt. 12:28; 11:5; 12:41-42; 13:16-17).[17]
Thus Jesus' preaching paradoxically places man between two
"final" focal points. Fuchs[18] and Conzelmann[19] prefer to say

[16] The efforts of scholars like J. Arthur Baird (*The Justice of God in the
Teaching of Jesus*, pp. 77–79, 81–82, 94, 102, 112, 145–151) and Ethelbert
Stauffer ("The Relevance of the Historical Jesus," in *The Historical Jesus
and the Kerygmatic Christ*, pp. 47–48) to deny that Jesus as a man of his
day used apocalyptic thought forms will hardly stand up in the face of such
exegetical demonstrations as that of W. G. Kümmel, *Promise and Fulfil-
ment*, trans. D. M. Barton ("Studies in Biblical Theology," No. 23 [London:
SCM Press, 1957]). Norman Perrin concedes that the kingdom is an apocalyptic concept in Jesus' teaching but qualifies this to the point that little or
nothing remains of the apocalyptic (*The Kingdom of God in the Teaching
of Jesus*, pp. 158, 177–178, 185–190). According to Käsemann, Jesus proclaimed the coming of the kingdom of God, but Jesus did not speak of it
exclusively or even primarily as the chronologically datable end of the world.
Rather, for Jesus the kingdom meant God's becoming immediately present
for man. In Käsemann's view the non-apocalyptic character of Jesus' preaching distinguished it from the message of John the Baptist, on the one hand,
and from the kerygma of the earliest Jewish-Christian church on the other;
and Käsemann uses quotation marks even in speaking of Jesus' "eschatology."
See Ernst Käsemann, "Zum Thema der urchristlichen Apokalyptik," *Zeitschrift für Theologie und Kirche*, 59 (1962), 260–263.
[17] James M. Robinson ("The Formal Structure of Jesus' Message," p. 97)
has stated that Bultmann and C. H. Dodd have moved closer together in
recent years, Bultmann relinquishing some of his emphasis on futuristic
eschatology in favor of recognizing that Jesus also proclaimed an eschatological present, and Dodd relinquishing some of his emphasis on realized
eschatology in favor of an eschatology in the process of realization. Robinson
is probably right with reference to Bultmann. Cf. Bultmann, "Man between
the Times According to the New Testament," p. 253; "The Primitive Christian Kerygma and the Historical Jesus," in *The Historical Jesus and the
Kerygmatic Christ*, p. 29. But with respect to Dodd, though in a footnote
he expresses approval of "sich realisierende Eschatologie" (*The Interpretation of the Fourth Gospel* [Cambridge: The University Press, 1953], p. 447),
in the revised edition of *The Parables of the Kingdom* (1961) he gives no
indication of abandoning realized eschatology; cf. pp. viii, 29–35, 159, 167.
[18] *Historical Jesus*, pp. 137–138, 158.
[19] "Life of Jesus," p. 64.

that Jesus saw himself as a sign of the kingdom and his time as the time of calling for the kingdom rather than that Jesus saw his ministry as the actual advent of the kingdom. Käsemann, on the other hand, states that Jesus saw the coming of the kingdom in his word.[20] As Dahl has suggested, more important than the terminology are the meaning and relationship of the two focal points.[21] However, such texts as Matt. 12:28 seem to indicate that Jesus saw his own time as the time of the *kingdom's* coming.

The essentially mythological nature of the apocalyptic expectation, along with its failure to materialize, requires a translation into existentialist terms, and such a translation yields an understanding of existence in history. The juxtaposition of sayings expressing both realized and futuristic eschatology suggests that present and future are inherently related. Each is seen in the light of the other, and human existence is a movement from the present to the future. The eschatological element points to the cruciality and urgency of the decision which man is called upon to make in the present and asserts that the challenge comes to man from beyond himself and that its future outcome is not finally subject to man's manipulation. The futuristic eschatological sayings present the kingdom of God as holding open the possibility of man's being finally saved or lost. When the present is seen in the light of this future, it takes on the character of a challenge to decision and also an anticipation of the final outcome. When the future kingdom is seen in the light of the fullness of life and renewal in the present, then the future becomes the completion of something already begun. Because the kingdom of God is fu-

---

[20] *Essays on New Testament Themes*, pp. 43–44. Fuchs (*Historical Jesus*, p. 106, n. 1) says that he agrees with this statement of Käsemann despite his (Fuchs') hesitation elsewhere to speak of Jesus' seeing the kingdom as actually coming in his ministry.

[21] "Parables," p. 157.

ture, man is waiting; but because it is also present, the man who responds is fulfilled. The man who lives the existence envisioned by Jesus' eschatology both has and has not; thus he is man in movement, in movement toward having what he has; being is becoming.

What is the relationship of the parables to Jesus' eschatology? It is not that certain elements in the parables simply point to the two focal points of Jesus' eschatology in a direct or allegorical way. That is, for example, the master's giving the talents to his servants does not point·directly to Jesus' earthly ministry with the master's return pointing to the future consummation and the Parousia of the Son of Man. Rather the understanding of existence implied in the mythological eschatology is given a different—and fuller—configuration in the parables. The content of this I have tried to suggest in chapters 4 and 5. To the extent that the parables reflect Jesus' eschatology, they *are* a demythologizing of it, or, more correctly, they are a pre-mythological and aesthetic expression of the existential intention of the eschatology. There is both a tension between and a rapprochement of, say, the one-talent man's loss of his talent or the five maidens' being shut out of the wedding feast and the mythological idea of the final judgment. The parables pull the ultimate loss of existence implied in the final judgment into a pattern of happening human existence so that the final judgment, the unrecoverable loss of existence, becomes an event in the midst of history. At the same time, because of the subsidiary connection between the ending of the parables and the non-parabolic eschatological sayings, the latter tend to pull the former out of the earthly continuum and to emphasize the finality of the loss and the presiding hand of God. We have seen, however, that the parables in their own way, independently of their connection with Jesus' non-parabolic eschatological sayings, indicate the eschatological crossing of the everyday.

Is the emphasis in Jesus' eschatology on the future or the present kingdom? Is the real center of gravity the future, so that the present is seen only in its light, as a crisis and at the most an anticipation? Or is the weight on the present and its rich actuality, so that the future is seen in its light, as the completion of something already very much begun? The parables may shed some light on this question although they do not give a conclusive answer. In The Ten Maidens and The Unjust Steward the future is the center of gravity. The young womens' activity is elicited almost altogether by the expectation of the future festal occasion, and the unjust steward acts entirely to ward off a future threat. The present is a crisis, a time for resolve and activity, because it is seen in the light of the future. It is ironical that the young women, who expect the best from the future, are shut out, while the unjust steward, who fears the worst, gains well-being.

In The Talents there is more or less equal emphasis on the two focal points. There is in the future, in part two of the parable, an accounting for the activity in which the servants are engaged in part one of the story, and the consequences of the activity and the accounting are drawn out in part three. But the servants are not expected to trade with their money simply in order to be held accountable in the future. One cannot avoid the future consequences of his present action, but taking the risk of opening oneself to one's largest possibilities and abandoning the restrictive security of non-action is a present good in itself; it is authentic existence. The present is seen in its own light as well as in the light of the future. This would also seem to be true of The Wicked Tenants.

In The Prodigal Son (and in The Workers in the Vineyard, The Unforgiving Servant, and The Wedding Garment) the center of gravity has shifted to the present. The emphasis is on the power of the present to evoke action or on the gift and demand which confront man in the present. The future in an

189

eschatological sense is implied in these parables very lightly. Certainly it is seen in the light of the present.

The preceding discussion suggests that neither thoroughgoing nor realized eschatology[22] will stand up in the light of the parables. Jesus' eschatology had two focal points, but if there was in Jesus' teaching an overarching and systematic view as to where the emphasis lay, it does not appear in the tradition which has come down to us.

3. The Parables and Jesus' Understanding of His Mission

It seems to be clear that Jesus did not speak of himself as the Messiah, and the question whether he used any broadly "messianic" titles of himself, including Son of Man, remains an unsolved, and perhaps insoluble, problem. Quite apart from literary, historical, and theological considerations, Ramsey has pointed out that it would be *logically* impossible for Jesus to be "the Messiah" since mysterious situations cannot be spoken about in straightforward language.[23] Ramsey, however, argues for the historicity of Jesus' using the term Son of Man on the ground that his employment of it is appropriately problematic and enigmatic.[24]

[22] The criticism of Dodd's realized eschatology given by Reginald Fuller, which says that Dodd's view destroys "the cruciality of the cross," seems beside the point. Cf. Reginald H. Fuller, *The Mission and Achievement of Jesus* ("Studies in Biblical Theology," No. 12 [London: SCM Press, 1954]), pp. 48–49. For Dodd the realized eschatological event was a developing crisis which included Jesus' death and resurrection as well as the destruction of Jerusalem. Cf. *Parables* (1952, Nisbet ed.), pp. 75–80, 165; *Parables* (rev. ed.), pp. 50–59, 73, 82, 131. A more pertinent criticism of realized eschatology is that it tends to remove Christian existence from history. Christian existence becomes, not a movement from present to future through a history which is crossed in a hidden and mysterious way by the transcendent, but rather a movement out of history toward a spatially conceived transcendent. On the other hand, the existential implications of Dodd's view of a developing crisis would not be very different from the existential implications of realized and futuristic eschatology in juxtaposition. This, however, seems not to have been developed by Dodd.

[23] Ian T. Ramsey, *Religious Language*, p. 145.
[24] *Ibid.*, pp. 162–167.

Whatever the answer may be to the question of Jesus' use of titles, there is widespread agreement that his understanding of his mission burst the limits of the available Jewish categories and that he thought of himself as the eschatological person in some sense.[25] Jesus did not make his eschatological claim openly and directly but let it be absorbed in his work and words and expressed indirectly in his gracious association with sinners and his call to discipleship, in his free attitude toward the law as it stood and in his "but I say unto you," in his radicalizing of the demand of God. Conjointly his indirectly expressed eschatological awareness was reflected in the appeals of the sick and possessed, in the hopes of his followers, in the opposition of the Jewish leaders, and finally in his crucifixion.[26]

In view of the above it seems too much to say, as B. T. D. Smith[27] does, that none of the genuine parables throws any light on Jesus' conception of his relationship to the kingdom of God. We would expect an implicit Christology in the parables,[28] as in the other aspects of Jesus' ministry. Since the parables reflect in their own way the eschatology of Jesus' nonparabolic teaching and point subsidiarily to his historical situation, it may be said that they point subsidiarily to Jesus as the one who brings the situation which is dramatically and imaginatively portrayed in the parables. Jesus is the one who confronts men with the decisive crisis of their lives and offers the possibilities and understanding of existence which the parables present. It is, however, the meaning of a parable as a whole which points to the meaning of Jesus' ministry rather than some individual element in the parable that points directly and allegorically to Jesus.

---

[25] Cf., for example, Käsemann, *New Testament Themes*, pp. 38–44.
[26] Cf. Bornkamm, *Jesus of Nazareth*, p. 170; Conzelmann, "Life of Jesus," p. 67; Herbert Braun, "Der Sinn der neutestamentlichen Christologie," p. 347.
[27] *The Parables of the Synoptic Gospels*, p. 86.
[28] Cf. Dahl, "Parables," p. 158.

If the parables in their particular way give an account of what happens in Jesus' ministry and also point to the nature of God's act, then Jesus in the parables is implicitly claiming that his behavior is God's deed.[29] The grounds on which this statement can be made, however, need to be clarified somewhat further. As we have seen, the parables themselves, by the use of the surprising and improbable, suggest the impingement of the divine upon human existence. Moreover, when the parables are considered in connection with the non-parabolic proclamation of the kingdom of God, the king-master-father figure points still more explicitly to God. But in order to say that the parables also interpret Jesus' ministry and therefore implicitly identify his ministry with the deed of God we need to know something about Jesus' ministry from sources other than the parables themselves. That is, for example, unless we knew something about Jesus' association with the sinners and his conflict with Jewish legalism, we would not be led to think that the father's relationship with the prodigal son and his older brother reflected Jesus' relationship with sinners, on the one hand, and Pharisees, on the other. The parables present their own autonomous world and make sense in themselves, but because we know enough about Jesus' ministry outside of the parables to notice their subsidiary pointing to his situation, they become for us interpretations of that event.

Jesus' behavior, which challenged the Jewish world of fixed religious values, precipitated a conflict that resulted in his death. Inasmuch as his parables are interpretations of his behavior, they are a part of the provocation of his conflict; hence he risked his life through his word.[30] Since his word is an inter-

---

[29] Cf. Jeremias, *Parables*, pp. 37–38; Eta Linnemann, *Die Gleichnisse Jesu*, p. 93; Bornkamm, *Jesus*, p. 81; Fuchs, *Historical Jesus*, pp. 21–22, 36–37.

[30] Cf. Linnemann, *Gleichnisse*, pp. 48–49; Fuchs, *Historical Jesus*, pp. 21, 37.

pretation of the life which issued organically in death, it is also an interpretation of his death: the one who lives the kind of existence which the parables urge will die, but his loss of life is really the gaining of life.

My argument has been moving toward the assertion that the decision which Jesus called on men to make in favor of faith or authentic existence was a decision which he had made himself.[31] Since the parables present a picture of the difference between authentic and inauthentic existence, they make some suggestion to us about what Jesus affirmed and what he rejected. In view of the fact that the parables are regarded as basically genuine by a consensus of New Testament scholarship, and if it can be supposed that there is some continuity between what Jesus demanded of others and what he decided for himself, then it can hardly be denied that the parables are a clue to Jesus' understanding of his own existence. This does not mean, in view of the relative autonomy and imaginative configuration of the aesthetic object, that the existential understanding implied in the parables and Jesus' understanding of his own existence are identical. Nor does it mean, again, that individual elements in the parables point directly and allegorically to Jesus. But it does mean that there is some continuity between the understanding of existence implied in the parables and Jesus' understanding of himself.

If Jesus interpreted his ministry as the deed of God, then the faith or understanding of existence out of which his actions or words proceeded is also a very significant dimension of God's deed. One could say that the coming of the kingdom is the possibility of faith's coming to man from beyond himself—as an act of God—and Jesus is the model for that faith. The parables, as we noted above, are indirect clues to the content of

[31] Cf. Gerhard Ebeling, *Word and Faith*, pp. 201–202, 204–206, 234, 238, 295; Fuchs, *Historical Jesus*, pp. 23, 30, 62, 80; Gloege, *Day*, pp. 126, 223.

Jesus' faith, and they present imaginative configurations of various aspects of that faith and of how it—or its opposite—might manifest itself. The parables confront a man as a language event, calling him to decision and opening up the possibility of a new world—a real present, moving toward a real future, in which there is time to gain a unified existence under the gift and demand of God. The language event is the indirect expression of Jesus' faith as a possibility for other men.

Does this mean that Jesus perfectly realized faith or authentic existence? Did he actualize the existence which his tragic characters failed to actualize and which the prodigal son actualized only partially in his coming from death to life? Did Jesus risk renouncing utterly both self-protective non-action and self-assertive action? Did he repudiate all self-contrived security and depend absolutely on the sustaining power of the gracious but hidden Father who can bring life out of death? And did Jesus give himself utterly for the sake of others? Was his existence perfectly unified in that he responded without reserve to both the gift and the demand of God, in that he lived with complete appropriateness to the situation to which he had been called?

Van Harvey and Schubert Ogden have criticized James Robinson for making the theological significance of Jesus consist in the fact that Jesus actualized authentic existence and for holding that only on the ground of Jesus' actualization of it is authentic existence a possibility for others.[32] The bases of their criticism are as follows: (a) Such a position as Robinson's raises doubts about the reliability of the kerygma for salvation and creates an anxiety that wants to prove the kerygma by the investigation of Jesus' history.[33] (b) We do not have sufficient

[32] Van A. Harvey and Schubert M. Ogden, "How New Is the 'New Quest of the Historical Jesus'?" in *The Historical Jesus and the Kerygmatic Christ*, pp. 221–222, 231–232.

[33] *Ibid.*, pp. 231–234.

biographical information about Jesus to establish that he always maintained authentic existence.[34] (c) It is in principle impossible to establish a man's faith and whether he actualized it by observing his words and deeds. Faith is hidden.[35] In opposition to Robinson, Harvey and Ogden maintain that it need not and cannot be decided whether Jesus *actualized* existence in faith. It only needs to be said that his word with unequaled force presents us with the demand for decision and that Jesus *represents* authentic existence.[36]

In response to Harvey and Ogden it should be said that the discounting of the quest of the historical Jesus on the ground that it might create anxiety about the kerygma is itself an expression of anxiety. In their second and third points noted above, however, they seem to be right. Jesus' association with

[34] *Ibid.*, pp. 236–237, 241.

[35] *Ibid.*, pp. 238–239; Harvey, "The Historical Jesus, the Kerygma, and the Christian Faith," pp. 440–441. Cf. also Dilthey, *Pattern*, p. 116; Van Buren, *Secular*, p. 53.

[36] Schubert M. Ogden, *Christ without Myth* (New York: Harper, 1961), pp. 161–164; Harvey, "Historical Jesus," pp. 447–448. Also for Bultmann the question of whether Jesus actualized authentic existence is a matter of indifference. The significant thing about Jesus is that he was the bearer of the word, and if he was not the bearer of the word that would not change the word's significance (*Jesus and the Word*, pp. 14, 217). For Bultmann the important thing about the incarnation is that revelation should occur as an encounter, as a language event (*Jesus*, pp. 4, 6, 8, 11; "Jesus and Paul," in *Existence and Faith*, pp. 194–196; "The Case for Demythologizing," pp. 191–193). But for Bultmann authentic existence comes through encounter with the *Christian kerygma* and is not generally available ("New Testament and Mythology," pp. 26–33; "The Question of Natural Revelation," in *Essays Philosophical and Theological*, pp. 94, 98, 109–114) despite the fact that it does not depend on Jesus' having realized authentic existence. It may be noticed that in *Jesus and the Word* (pp. 6, 10, 11) Bultmann spoke of the possibility of an existential encounter with Jesus' word, and in "Jesus and Paul" he emphasized the continuity between the teaching of those two. But in the more recent "The Primitive Christian Kerygma" he denies that the word of the historical Jesus really reaches us existentially, as salvation (pp. 30, 40–41), and he emphasizes the discontinuity between Jesus and the kerygma (pp. 20–30). The change between the earlier and later works does not represent a reversal, but it is a real shift of emphasis. It seems that Bultmann by reaction to the new quest has become more negative in his attitude toward the historical Jesus than he formerly was.

sinners and his willingness to enter into conflict and to suffer
do suggest a certain continuity between his existence and the
understanding of existence contained in his teaching. But to
prove from texts that he perfectly actualized his understanding
of existence is impossible both in principle and in practice.

Let us look further at Robinson's position, however, specifically at three assertions which he makes: (a) The quest of the
historical Jesus cannot prove that God acted in Jesus' intentions or that Jesus actually lived out of transcendence.[37] (b)
Jesus—his selfhood and understanding of existence—can be
encountered through modern historiography as well as in the
kerygma.[38] (c) Jesus did actualize authentic or eschatological
existence, that is, live out of transcendence, and the cross "must
be interpreted" as the climax of that actualization.[39]

When Robinson says that the new quest makes an encounter
with Jesus' selfhood available, he must mean—or could only
properly mean—that the new quest as a hermeneutical endeavor on the New Testament texts makes Jesus' understanding of existence a language event for me. I am put in the
position of having to make a decision. This does not and cannot prove, however, that Jesus actualized authentic existence,
which Robinson concedes (point (a) above). Why then does
he state that Jesus' existence "must" be interpreted as the
actualization of authentic existence? Robinson does not make
this clear, but I believe that it can be made clear. It can be
argued that Jesus' actualization of authentic existence is a
necessary theological reflection on the experience of faith in
view of the biblical understanding of man's radical implication
in evil—in inauthenticity. Faith needs to say only that Jesus is
the bringer of faith or new life or authenticity; but when we re-

[37] James M. Robinson, A New Quest of the Historical Jesus ("Studies in
Biblical Theology," No. 25 [London: SCM Press, 1959]), pp. 77, 94.
[38] Ibid., pp. 94, 105.
[39] Ibid., pp. 89, 108; Robinson, "Formal," pp. 99, 104.

flect on this new life in the light of what our plight was, we are brought to say that deliverance could take place, authenticity could be really possible for us, only if authentic existence actually occurred, was perfectly realized, and not just represented, at some point in history. The power of inauthenticity could be broken only by the concrete actualization of authenticity. The view which says that the redemptive event need only have been a representation of authentic existence necessarily entails a less radical view of man's implication in evil.

The affirmation that Jesus perfectly actualized existence in faith is neither a statement of faith nor a provable inference from historical texts. Jesus' actualization is rather a theological reflection and as such is a metaphysical fact. A metaphysical system is not intended to correspond literally to reality as a whole, but it is designed to provide coherence and a meaningful context for all facts and explanations. A metaphysical fact is a crucial concept without which the system would not hold together,[40] and it is subject to the kind of verification which is appropriate to metaphysical statements and systems.

If I may now summarize the conclusions of this section:

The eschatological coming of the kingdom of God is Jesus' faith as a model for our faith. The parables are the richest expression of the faith which Jesus called men to, and, on the assumption that his own decision lay behind the decision he asked of others, an important clue to the content of Jesus' faith. That Jesus perfectly actualized this faith is for the Christian perspective a metaphysical fact.

It now remains to raise the question as to the ultimate source of the parables' power to be a language event which is the eschatological event.[41]

---

[40] Frederick Ferré, *Language, Logic, and God*, p. 161; *Exploring the Logic of Faith*, p. 74.

[41] There is no contradiction between saying that Jesus' faith is the eschatological event and the parables are the eschatological event, because Jesus' faith meets us in his words.

4. The Language Event and the Event of the Resurrection

It is possible to hold that the power of Jesus' parables resides in the primary traits of language itself. According to
Linnemann, when a speaker is involved in a conflict which
reaches the depths of existence, as Jesus was in the controversy
with his opponents, he can only turn to the power of language.
Linnemann makes reference to Heidegger's position that it is
language which speaks, and man speaks insofar as he hears and
responds to the speaking of language.[42] From this standpoint
the weight of Jesus' words was wholly in the words themselves,
and who Jesus was for his hearers depended entirely on what he
became for them through his word.[43] Fuchs similarly maintains
that Jesus wanted to justify himself solely on the ground of his
preaching. Jesus did demand of men a decision about his person (Mark 8:38), but he wanted to be understood in and not
apart from his proclamation. "He understood himself as the
witness of a new situation."[44]

Again, if it is held that language is its own source of power,
the resurrection of Jesus can be identified, almost without remainder, with the effective proclamation of the resurrection.
"Jesus has risen in the kerygma."[45] This amounts to saying
that the resurrection is the power of the kerygma to grasp us,[46]
and it must be acknowledged that to a degree, at least, the
resurrection *is* the kerygma. The remainder which keeps the
identification from being complete, according to this viewpoint,
is that the resurrection can also be identified, as Bultmann
would have it, with the disciples' coming to faith.[47] To ask
modern man to believe something as incredible as the resusci-

[42] Linnemann, *Gleichnisse*, p. 40
[43] *Ibid.*, p. 43.
[44] Fuchs, *Historical Jesus*, p. 224.
[45] Bultmann, "The Primitive Christian Kerygma," p. 42.
[46] Cf. Fuchs, *Historical Jesus*, p. 38; Bultmann, "Mythology," pp. 41–42.
[47] Bultmann, "Mythology," p. 42.

tation of a corpse is to ask him to believe something because it is in the Bible that he would not be asked to believe if it were related in any other source.[48] Or if modern man is really not so troubled by the scientific problem, there are the discrepancies in the Easter stories themselves.[49] But if the resurrection is understood as the rise of the disciples' faith in Jesus, then it can be proclaimed convincingly and joyfully.[50] Faith arises from an encounter with the proclamation of the resurrection; thus the language event and the rise of faith come to be two sides of the same reality—the resurrection event, which is identified without remainder with language-event-plus-faith.

But we must now raise the question whether the primary traits of language itself can explain the power of the kerygma and the rise of faith in Jesus and whether such an explanation would be faithful to the New Testament. To be sure language itself has power without being the expression of a particular historical reality, which is seen in the fact that mythology, poetry, and fiction may have great power over people although they express the hypothetical and potential rather than the historical. By the same token part of the explanation of the power of the New Testament's language is the meaning expressed in the linguistic structures, apart from their reference to history. But does this exhaust the New Testament's understanding?

It would seem that for Heidegger language is not powerful simply as language, but it is powerful when it is the happening of being, when it is called forth by being as primal thought to show that beings are.[51] We might say that for the New

---

[48] Cf. Bultmann, "Mythology," pp. 38–39; Gerhard Ebeling, *The Nature of Faith*, trans. R. G. Smith (Philadelphia: Muhlenberg Press, 1961), pp. 46, 61.

[49] Cf. Anderson, *Jesus*, p. 187.

[50] Ebeling, *Faith*, pp. 62–63; *Word and Faith*, pp. 301–302.

[51] Cf. James M. Robinson, *The Later Heidegger and Theology*, pp. 25, 44, 49–50.

Testament its language is powerful because of its connection with a concrete and particular happening. The kerygma is effective because of its relationship to something which cannot be exhausted by language-plus-faith. Laeuchli's point, that to identify Christ with speech about him is idolatrous, seems to be well taken.[52]

Is there any way out of the circle that the language about the resurrection produced faith in it and faith in it produced the proclamation? Is there a reality that lay behind both the faith and the language? If that reality were Jesus' historical ministry alone, why did his death cause the disciples to lose faith and what overcame their depression and convinced them that Jesus was victorious after all?

A number of contemporary scholars have been concerned to understand the resurrection of Jesus as something more than a derivative from the faith-experience of the earliest community,[53] but not as much clarity as one could hope for has been achieved in saying what it was. This is largely due to the inherent difficulty of the problem, for it must be agreed that the New Testament's understanding of the resurrection as an eschatological event and the discrepancies among the appearance stories put the task beyond the historian's tools. Should more be done in the way of an ontological understanding? I should like to offer one possible line of thought, and Brevard Childs' understanding of the Old Testament theology of history has been quite suggestive here.

In the Old Testament understanding of history an event of the past may be actualized in the present through memory, as

[52] Samuel Laeuchli, *The Language of Faith*, p. 235.

[53] Richard R. Niebuhr, *Resurrection and Historical Reason* (New York: Scribner's, 1957), pp. 145–146, 172–181; Anderson, *Jesus*, pp. 202–203, 237, 240; Bornkamm, *Jesus*, pp. 180–185; "Myth and Gospel: A Discussion of the Problem of Demythologizing the New Testament Message," in *Kerygma and History*, pp. 177, 193–195; Van Buren, *Secular*, pp. 124–126, 128, 132–133.

new responses are called forth.[54] Actualization does not mean
that the past event is repeated or reenacted in the present as
would be the case in a typically mythological outlook. Rather
in the Old Testament *historical* events are actualized, and historical events are non-repeatable, once-for-all, and fixed in a
chronological sequence. If the past event cannot be brought
into the present, neither can the worshiper be taken out of the
present and united with a past event. What the Old Testament does affirm is that historical events may be the vehicle
for a quality of existence or a continuing reality which can
occur in later events. The exodus from Egypt cannot be repeated, but through the exodus there entered into history a
quality of existence in which later generations can participate.
The past event is actualized in the present through the recur-
rence of the same quality of existence or redemptive reality,
not through the repetition of the event.[55]

In a similar manner Amos Wilder has suggested that the
New Testament stories place us in the midst of the great plot
of all time and space and thus relate us to the great storyteller
—God. Plots overlap and play themselves over again in many
lives, but there is no literal identity or repetition, and each
time the plot occurs in an unprecedented way. Both sides of
this are seen in Gal. 2:20[56] and in the "I though not I" of
I Cor. 15:10. The life of existence in faith is *my* life lived in
this corporeal world, but it is also a participation in the crucifixion of Christ, who lives in me. That is, I share in the quality
of existence which came into history in Jesus' earthly life, and
the continuing availability of that quality is the resurrection.

If the power of biblical history—and especially the ministry
of Jesus—resides entirely in language's becoming an event, then

[54] Brevard S. Childs, *Memory and Tradition in Israel* ("Studies in Biblical
Theology," No. 37 [London: SCM Press, 1962]), pp. 51–54, 63.
[55] *Ibid.*, pp. 81–85.
[56] Wilder, *Rhetoric*, pp. 65–66.

the history is really inconsequential and a myth would serve just as well as history as the origin of the New Testament's language. Furthermore, if the language is held to be powerful on the ground that it is *about* the event, it could just as well be about an event which might have happened but did not. But in the New Testament it is of the utmost importance that the ministry of Jesus did happen. It opened up new possibilities in history: the rule of God dawned; acceptance by God came; Adam's disobedience was overcome; the light shone; access to God became available. At the same time Jesus' ministry as a historical event remains fixed in the past, and salvation occurs through encounter with the proclamation of the event (Rom. 1:16; I Cor. 1:18; II Cor. 5:18-20; 6:2; John 5:24; 17:8, 20). If salvation occurs through the proclaimed word and also has an unyielding connection with an event which remains in the past, then there must be a connection between the present word and the past event. The connecting link is the quality of existence which came into history through Jesus' ministry but which is not limited to that event. This reality is not a discarnate thing out there in mythological space but occurs only incarnately in the sacraments, in acts of faith, and in language. Thus Christian language has the power to be the eschatological language event when it becomes the "body" of this quality of existence. Perhaps we should say that while the existential reality gives to language its power, this can be affirmed only after language has put us in touch with the reality.

This continuing quality of existence, as suggested above, is what the New Testament means by the resurrection of Jesus. The resurrection understood in this way is a metaphysical fact, the extension and completion of Jesus' actualization of existence in faith. Why did the disciples proclaim anything at all about Jesus after his death? Assuming that his death divested them of whatever eschatological hopes they might have had, they were enlivened again to faith and hope precisely because

202

his death gave a resurgence of power to the quality of existence which came with his ministry. His death did this because it was the last and complete manifestation of his living his life out of transcendence rather than out of tangible security; therefore, because his actualization of existence in faith came about only as the living out to the end of a real life, his quality of existence could not attain its full power until his life was completed in death. The resurrection was his quality of existence attaining full power through death. This way of understanding Jesus' resurrection enables us to recognize the difference which it made in the disciples while acknowledging that Jesus' unique quality of existence was already occurring during his historical ministry.

The resurrection as a metaphysical or ontological fact, as the completion of Jesus' actualization of authentic existence, is not to be identified with the resuscitation of a corpse nor identified in any one-for-one fashion with the resurrection stories related in the Gospels. It is rather that Jesus' quality of existence, the kind of existence which the parables affirm, grasped the disciples and brought them to faith. Because the possibility of the disciples' new faith had such an unyielding connection with Jesus' having actualized existence in faith, they experienced their coming to faith as Jesus' presence or as faith in his resurrection. We may say then that the ontological event which was the faith of Jesus grasping the disciples—that is, Jesus' resurrection—produced their faith in his resurrection. Their faith produced visions of his appearance and the resurrection message. The resurrection stories in the Gospels are the fruition of the church's imaginative dealing with the resurrection kerygma and the resurrection visions.

At this juncture I would conclude that the resurrection reality may use the narrative language of the Synoptic Gospels—both stories about and by Jesus—as well as the more explicitly kerygmatic materials of the New Testament to reach us existentially in the present. In fact a neglect of the concrete language of the Synoptics and of their concern with Jesus' history would cause the linguistic body of the resurrection reality to become truncated and impersonal.[57] With reference to Jesus' own use of the parables, their power would have resided not only in their linguistic qualities but also in their being the expression of his being.

That a new quality of existence came to birth in concrete connection with Jesus' ministry and is also detachable from that fixed position in history is formally analogous to the fact that the parables are peculiarly related to Jesus but also have a certain independence of him. They bear the unique stamp of his imagination in a way that his other sayings do not, and they dramatize the existential situation which he brings and are a part of that situation's coming to language. Yet as aesthetic objects they have a relative autonomy and detach themselves from his history in a way that the other sayings do not. Paradoxically, as artistic creations, the parables are more intimately Jesus' own than are his other sayings, and at the same time they are more detached from him. They are more detached because the very power of language causes the artist especially to say more than he knows and because the parables belong not only to the history of the covenant people and the history of salvation but to the artistic tradition as well. These considerations may mean that the parables are particularly fit for being expressions of the new existential reality and for being the instruments through which it becomes a language event.

In this chapter we have considered the parables in relation to the Gospels, and in this connection we have noticed the power which linguistic structures themselves have to inform existence. Attention was then turned to the history with which

[57] For a fuller treatment of this position cf. my article "The Necessary Complement to the Kerygma," *The Journal of Religion*, 45 (1965), 30–38.

the Gospels are concerned and to the ontological implications and significance of that history. The parables offer some help in interpreting Jesus' eschatology at the conceptual level, but, more importantly, they are an independent and richer expression of the intention of his explicit eschatology. Furthermore, the parables portray the existence in faith to which Jesus calls men and offer a clue to the content of Jesus' own faith. In view of this and in view of the fact that the resurrection is the faith of Jesus grasping us, then the parables are a clue to what it means to live the resurrection existence. To live the resurrection existence is to be enabled by the continuing power of Jesus' faith to live the kind of existence which the parables call us to either by portraying it or by portraying its opposite. To acknowledge that an event of the past may actualize itself in our history is to recognize that history can transcend itself or to confess that the transcendent God uses history for his redemptive purpose but without violating history.

The discussion has moved from the literary to the historical to the ontological, and that is the way, I take it, that Christian existence moves. We are grasped first by the language of the gospel and then we are referred to the history from which it arose and to the ultimate significance of the history. That does not mean, however, that language is only a kind of preliminary stage which can be dispensed with once we have arrived at the other levels. The language of the gospel, along with its translation, continues to be the vehicle through which redemptive history and ultimate reality meet us and which gives structure and meaning to our own historical reality.

"Jesus came preaching. . . . And he taught them many things in parables. . . . My words will not pass away."

INDEXES

Index of Parables

Index of Biblical Passages

General Index

211

14, 115, 123 n. 30, 124 n. 32,
133 n. 49, 138 n. 60, 138 n. 61,
139 n. 64, 143 n. 70, 148 n. 9,
148 n. 10, 149 n. 12, 149 n. 13,
149 n. 15, 150 n. 18, 153 n. 22,
154 n. 23, 156, 158 n. 34,
163 n. 40, 164 n. 42, 164 n. 45,
169 n. 56, 183 n. 10, 192 n. 29

Jesus, historical, 172–173, 183–187,
190–197, 198, 202, 203
quest for 49 n. 63, 183–185,
194–197
resurrection of, 180, 181, 198–205

Job, 146

Johnson, S., 8 n. 21, 10 n. 25

Jonas, H., 33

Jones, G. V., x, xi n. 7, 6 n. 16, 10 n.
28, 14 n. 36, 23, 46 n. 52, 90–
91, 99 n. 86, 105 n. 104, 169 n.
53

Jülicher, A., 2, 8, 14, 18, 24 n. 69

Kafka, F., 80

Kahler, E., 72 n. 10, 73 n. 12, 74 n.
13, 82 n. 37

Käsemann, E., 21, 22 n. 63, 186 n.
16, 187, 191 n. 25

Keast, W. R., 100 n. 92

Kerygma, 177–179, 183–185, 194,
195 n. 36, 196, 198–200, 202,
203

Killinger, J., 107

Kingdom of God, 52, 95, 104–105,
154, 193–194
See also Eschatology

Kitto, H. D. F., 112 n. 11, 112 n. 12

Klassen, W., 40 n. 37

Krieger, M., 71 n. 3, 77 n. 26, 78,
79, 81, 84–85, 93 n. 71, 94 n.
73, 147 n. 7

Kümmel, W. G., 186 n. 16

Laeuchli, S., 44, 49 n. 62, 65 n. 127,
100 n. 90, 200

Lampe, G. W. H., 43 n. 41

Language, and being, 50 n. 68, 198–
200, 202, 203–205
and historical reality, 30–33, 48,
85–86, 199–200, 204–205
how it expresses meaning, 71–73,
82, 86
its several functions, 35–36, 52–
53, 59, 63
and understanding, 32, 33–36,
43–44, 45, 48–49, 83, 86, 130–
131

Language event, 52–57, 65, 67, 85–
86, 94, 196, 197 n. 41, 199,
201–202, 204–205

Lewis, R. W. B., 147 n. 8, 172

Linguistic analysis, 52, 58–59

Linnemann, E., xi n. 5, xii, 2, 3 n.
3, 5, 7 n. 18, 12 n. 34, 12 n.
35, 19 n. 53, 24, 38 n. 11, 40 n.
36, 47 n. 55, 52 n. 74, 53 n. 76,
53 n. 77, 54–57, 89, 91, 95 n.
74, 105 n. 104, 106 n. 105,
123, 124 n. 33, 130 n. 42, 138,
139 n. 63, 140, 142 n. 67,
142 n. 69, 143 n. 72, 149 n.
11, 149 n. 12, 150 n. 19, 150 n.
20, 154 n. 25, 163 n. 40, 164 n.
42, 169, 170 n. 57, 172 n. 64,
192 n. 29, 192 n. 30, 198

Literary criticism (non-biblical), ix–
x, 10, 44, 84, 93–94
See also "New" criticism

Literary form, 44, 74–76, 89–92, 96,
99–100, 101, 116–117, 134,
140–141, 149–150, 181

Logical positivism, 57–58, 60 n. 104,
147

Macbeth, 136

MacIntyre, A., 58 n. 92, 58 n. 93,
58 n. 95, 59 n. 101, 59 n. 103,
61 n. 109, 67 n. 130, 68 n. 133

McNeile, A. H., 8 n. 21

217